Sweet **Hug**

Seasonal Desserts from around the World

By **Natasa Tsirmpa**

Photographs by **Natasa Tsirmpa**
Cover Design by **Vangelis Karakasis**

First edition: November 2021

ISBN 978-618-85730-0-0 hardcover
ISBN 978-618-85730-1-7 paperback

Natasa *works for a study abroad program of an American University in Greece.*
She cooks for the students and immensely enjoys introducing them to Greek cuisine
and to flavors that are "exotic" to them. This is her second cookbook.

Introduction

I was seven or eight years old when I was introduced to the magical world of baking. My mom and I went over to our neighbor's home for an errand. At the time, our neighbor Mrs. Mary was effortlessly shaping moustokouloura, a very popular kind of Greek cookie made with olive oil, cinnamon, cloves and moustos. Moustos is grape juice that is just starting the fermentation process (long before it becomes wine). I found myself walking into a magical world. The home was whiffling with the enticing aroma of cinnamon. The oven was gleaming with excitement as a batch of cookies was baking to perfection. And the kitchen table was mounted with the oily dough and cookie sheets, some empty, some full of artfully shaped cookies waiting their turn to go in the oven, and some filled with baked, aromatic, crunchy moustokouloura, calling me to try them. I stood there, spellbound, my jaw-dropping, my eyes wide open as at that moment I was introduced to an enchanting world; I was embarking on my lifelong love affair with pastry making...

Josie helped me with kneading this dough. I am so glad her parents,
Mac and Jenni, let her be my helper for the day.

My mother is an excellent cook. Her guests always taste a variety of exquisitely prepared dishes. However, she, like my daughters, does not like eating desserts, (I am not exactly sure how I fit in there) and she does not like weighing things and measuring, so her baking skills do not match her cooking accomplishments. Growing up we had this unspoken agreement: When we had guests, she cooked, and I baked. It worked well for both of us and gave me the excuse to start experimenting with new and exciting desserts very early. I also discovered that a good dessert will elevate any meal, and this empirical knowledge has been imprinted in me.

Acknowledgments

For the completion of this book, a lot of people supported me and went out of their way to contribute their expertise and to make sure I overcame the many difficulties and setbacks. I am deeply grateful for all of them.

Vangelis Karakasis has created a stunning cover and graphic design for the book.
Nikias Alexandris has taken some incredible pictures for this book. His pictures can be found on pages 3, 127, 129, 130, 131, 143, 171.
Aiden Haslam has done a fine job in editing the book.
My aunt Katerina Whitley, an accomplished author herself, also read and edited the book.
Special thanks to Noah Darnel for his valuable and pertinent input.

I want to thank my mom for letting me mess her kitchen regularly since I was ten or eleven years old.

The students who come to Greece with our study abroad program are a constant source of inspiration, joy and excitement for me. I am very grateful for them.
I want to thank especially the students who were in Greece in the summer of 2021 for the support and help they so fervently offered me. They came up with smart and funny quotes, hand-modeled whenever I asked for them, gave me input on recipes and shared their contagious joy and love with me. I hope they realize how grateful I am for each one of them!

Lastly, I want to thank my family for being there for me, for offering great ideas, constructive criticism and, most of all, unconditional love and support. Thank you!

This book is divided into six sections: The four seasons followed by Christmas and Easter. Every seasonal section includes twenty recipes: nineteen desserts and one savory treat. Christmas and Easter are slightly smaller.

I am a firm believer in the importance of consuming fruit at its prime. The taste of seasonal fruit that has been grown locally and matured on the tree is unparalleled. Using these tasteful fruits in desserts will yield exquisite pastries. Having said that, my recommendations for desserts in each season are just that, recommendations. A Mosaic (chocolate dessert, page 63) can be enjoyed throughout the year. But since we are consuming it cold, it is especially satisfying in the summer.

There are a lot of classic desserts in this cookbook, Greek, European, Middle Eastern, and a few American ones with a twist. There are several individual preparations combined in desserts that I hope you get to make and master. You can use your favorite preparations in creative combinations to invent your signature dessert.

It is my aspiration that I inspire you to experience the deep satisfaction and pure joy that derives from creating a dessert from scratch.

The number next to a dessert indicates servings for the listed amounts.

Gluten-free is marked next to the title of applicable dessert.

Dairy-free is marked next to the title of applicable dessert.

Techniques *used in this book*

Bain Marie. When we want to melt chocolate or pasteurize eggs, we use Bain Marie, also known as a water bath. We place our ingredients in a metal or glass bowl. We then place the bowl on top of a pot with simmering water and let the contents of the bowl melt or cook in the steam of the simmering water underneath. It is very important that the bottom of the metal or glass bowl mustn't touch the water of the pot at any point.

Gelatin. We use gelatin to thicken up a liquid or a cream. Using gelatin sounds intimidating until you understand how it works. Gelatin comes in two forms: a transparent plastic-looking sheet and a powder. To use either one you need to take two steps: 1. Add moisture to it and 2. Dissolve it. It is important to remember these two steps.

A) Gelatin sheets. Place the gelatin sheets in a small bowl with cold water. Three to ten minutes later, take the now-*moistened,* wiggly and transparent sheets out of the water. Squeeze the excess water off thoroughly (discard the water) and add the sheets into the warm liquid of your recipe. Mix very well to *dissolve* the gelatin.

B) Gelatin powder. Place a teaspoon of the powder in a cup with two tablespoons of water or other liquid such as milk or orange juice. Let it soak for a few minutes to absorb *moisture.* Then add it (along with the water or milk or orange juice) to the liquid you want to thicken to *dissolve* the gelatin. If the liquid you need to thicken is cold (yogurt), warm up the cup with the liquid and the gelatin powder in the microwave for 15-20 seconds first, and then add it to the liquid you want to thicken. Mix the gelatin with your liquid very well.
If your liquid is cold, we suggest you use powder gelatin and not gelatin sheets.

Dry Yeast. Always remember that salt kills dry yeast. So, when you are making dough and using yeast, the first thing to do is to add the yeast to a liquid with sugar (which feeds the yeast), whether the liquid mandated by the recipe is water or milk. Mix well and then you may add half the flour mentioned in the recipe. Mix again, and ***then*** add the salt with the rest of the flour. This way, you won't run the risk of killing your yeast.

Beurre Clarifié: means cleared butter which is achieved by melting unsalted butter over low heat. There are some remarkable benefits to using *beurre clarifié*. First, by melting the butter, the milk protein (casein) is separated from the fat, which means that lactose-intolerant people can eat the butter. Second, *beurre clarifié* has a higher burning point than butter. Therefore, it is preferable to use *beurre clarifié* instead of butter when we want to fry meat or fish. Third, it lasts longer than butter when kept in the fridge.
To make *beurre clarifié*, start by gently heating unsalted butter. Forming on the surface, there will be foam. When the foam subsides (which means the water of the butter has evaporated), remove the whey that is floating on the surface, with a slotted spoon. This is delicious, save it and use it on salads or pasta. You now need to remove the protein particles that have sunk to the bottom of the pot, by straining the melted butter through a fine sieve. You can store the butter in a clean jar. If you leave the butter on the stove a little longer and let it burn slightly, it takes on a golden color and a nutty aroma. It is then called **beurre noisette,** widely used in pastry making or as a sauce on vegetables or meat. Beurre noisette has a deep aroma that enhances the flavor in baking. I use it on my baklava or in cakes.

Chocolate; Tempering and Decorating

Start by buying the best cooking chocolate you can find, preferably 70-76% cocoa content. Taste a few brands and note when your cake has the richest flavor and best texture.

When you find your favorite chocolate start experimenting with tempering it. Have you ever had chocolate that looks shiny, feels snappy in your mouth, and does not melt on your fingers quickly? It is tempered chocolate. Tempered chocolate has the above characteristics because a number of its crystals are stabilized. To temper the chocolate and stabilize the crystals you need to melt it first, carefully, (either over a Bain Marie or in the microwave) and then cool it fast by stirring it. When the crystals are stabilized, the chocolate is too cool and thick to work with, so we need to warm it up again slightly (88-90°F); this keeps enough stabilized crystals to give the shiny, snappy effect but also brings the temperature to the point that allows you to work with it. Sounds complicated, right? If you try it, you will be surprised that you will end up with wonderful, silky chocolate. It helps if you have a candy thermometer, but you will do just fine without one if you pay attention. There are many methods to temper chocolate, here are the two I prefer:

1. Chop the chocolate roughly. Place it in a double boiler (Bain Marie) until it melts. Be very careful that no moisture from the bottom simmering pot enters the melting chocolate or the chocolate will be ruined. Remove the upper bowl from the double boiler, but keep the pan with the warm water on the stove. Place the bowl with the chocolate on a wet towel. This will help you work with a stable bowl, but will also help you lower the temperature faster. With a spatula, start mixing the chocolate in a circular movement (not necessarily constantly in the same direction) until the temperature starts to drop and the chocolate starts to thicken slightly. When the chocolate feels lukewarm to your fingers, or a thermometer reads 80-82°F, take it back to the double boiler over hot but not boiling water, for 6-8 seconds, stirring constantly until it warms up slightly again 88-90°F. It is now ready to be used. Remove the Bain Marie from the stove. As you are working you might need to return the tempered chocolate over the pot with the warm water later, to rewarm the chocolate slightly until you are finished.

2. Chop the chocolate roughly and add it to a Bain Marie to melt. When all has melted, turn the heat off and transfer 3/4 of the melted chocolate to another clean and cool bowl, keeping the 1/4 in the double boiler over warm, but not boiling, water. Temper 3/4 of the chocolate stirring it with a spatula with big steady movements until it starts to thicken and feels lukewarm to your finger. Then transfer the cooled, tempered chocolate back to the bowl with the 1/4 of the chocolate over the double boiler, stir it up, and remove from the heat. When we mix the two chocolates, the mixture retains enough stabilized crystals to be tempered, while at the same time maintaining the right temperature to work with.

Chocolate bowls. Place a toothpick in an ice cube mold with an interesting shape, fill

with water, and freeze. Dip the ice cube in melted and tempered chocolate briefly and then lift it. Dip it in the chocolate one more time and then place it on a platter and wait for the ice to melt. Because of the contact of the chocolate with the ice, the chocolate might develop white spots. Apply some olive oil or melted butter to the chocolate, and the white spots will disappear. See dessert on page 143. Another way to make these is with small balloons. Inflate each balloon and dip it in tempered chocolate a few times. Let it cool, and then carefully pinch and remove the balloon.

Chocolate leaves: Choose beautiful real leaves; wash and then dry them completely. Apply tempered chocolate with a brush in 2 or 3 thin layers. Let the chocolate cool completely, and very carefully peel the green leaves off the chocolate. Store the chocolate leaves in a single layer in the fridge in an airtight container. Chocolate leaves are very beautiful and can be used as a stunning decoration, but they tend to be fragile, so handle them with care.

Cream and Meringue

When a recipe calls for stiff cream or meringue, whip the cream (or meringue) until the peak barely leans over when you lift the whisk up. An easy way to tell if your cream is thick enough is to turn the bowl upside down. The cream should not move. If the recipe calls for a soft peak cream, the peak should be wiggly and lean heavily. Follow the specifications for each recipe.

To load a piping bag with cream or meringue, place the nozzle of your choice in a piping bag first and then place the bag in a big glass, with the nozzle tip looking up so that the cream does not spill out, as shown here. Fill the bag with a spatula.

Caramel

There are two kinds of caramel, dry and wet. Dry caramel is the caramel created by melting sugar alone. It is easy to make and generally foolproof but it can burn very easily and can go from golden, beautiful caramel to a burned, bitter, unusable one in seconds. Wet caramel is created when we melt sugar with water. With this one, it is easier to control the temperature and thus the burning, but it has a big disadvantage; it can crystalize easier. Crystallization is a chain reaction, which means that once it starts, you cannot stop it. It happens when a sugar particle crystalizes on the side of the pot and then falls into the caramel. To prevent this from happening we can do a few things. 1) Apply oil to the sides of the pot before starting the caramel. 2) Add a couple drops of lemon juice to the caramel. 3) Brush the inside walls of the pot with water as soon as the boiling begins. 4) Use a heavy saucepan to make the caramel, in which case the sides are at an angle and not perpendicular to the caramel. 5) Add a little glucose to your syrup. If, despite your precautions, crystallization does happen, just throw the caramel away, and start all over again. I highly recommend buying a candy thermometer. It is a game-changer in caramel and pastry making.

Basic Caramel: 1 cup sugar + 1/4 cup distilled or bottled water + 2 or 3 drops of lemon juice. In a pot add all ingredients and mix. With a wet brush wash down the insides of the pot. Bring over medium heat and wait until the mixture starts to melt. If the sugar starts to darken in places, swirl the pan around, ever so slightly, to mix, and brush the insides of the pan with water immediately. It is important to control the temperature of the pan by lifting it off the heat for a few seconds as needed. When the caramel turns amber, pour it onto parchment paper or aluminum foil, or use it according to the recipe. When it is completely cool, you can break the caramel into smaller pieces. Or, while the caramel is still hot, you may score it with a buttered knife. Be very careful because fresh caramel is extremely hot.

One of the favorite things with our students is **caramelized nuts** (recipe on pages 59, 188).

Measurements

Dessert-making requires more accuracy than other types of cooking or baking. The most accurate way to measure your ingredients is by weighing them. It is also the easiest: you place a bowl on your scale, hit zero to eliminate the weight of the bowl, and then add your ingredients into the bowl. Cup measuring can be tricky because it is affected by the way you fill the cup by compressing the powders (flour, powdered sugar) or by not leveling the top of your ingredients correctly: this affects the amounts you use thus altering the consistency of your preparation. If you must measure in cups, use the liquid measuring cup to measure liquids and the dry measuring cup to measure solids.

Organization

One of the most important attributes of a successful cook is organization. Some preparations take a long time to make or need time to mature or cool. Make these first. Other preparations need to be used immediately after they are made. Some desserts can be made in fifteen minutes (semolina Halva), and then some desserts need two days to mature (Cannelé). Read the recipe carefully before you start baking. Knowing what you are getting into when you start making a dessert is very important and can shield you from major disappointment.

Chocolate candy, cakes, cookies, brownies, and **Baklava** will take about thirty minutes to make, 40-60 minutes to bake (except the chocolate candy) and they are ready.
Cakes with glazing, tarts, and layered desserts like **Mille Feuille, Charlotte, cupcakes,** and **Crostadas** require multiple preparations and need a bigger commitment of your time, usually two or three hours or even more.
Creams, Mousses, Puddings, Jellos, and Pavlovas need to stay in the fridge or in the oven to cool, or bake, for hours or overnight but do not require a big commitment of your time.
Cannelé and Madeleine need to mature in the fridge before you bake them.
Once you whisk up **whipped cream,** you need to use it immediately. The same is true for **mirror glazing** or **buttercreams** and **Italian meringue.**

Useful Tools

If you want to get serious about baking, it will be helpful to have a whisk, rubber spatula, bowls of different sizes, a rolling pin, pans, pots, cake forms (round and loaf ones), pie dishes, and silicone molds. Silicone molds are necessary for small cakes, like Cannelé, Madeline and Financier. Also, piping bags and a few nozzles are very useful and will assist you with producing impressive desserts.

A handheld mixer, stand mixer, handheld blender, food processor, digital scales, and a candy thermometer are used frequently. The first four can substitute for one another sufficiently in most cases, so even if you don't own all of them, you can still work around it.

Spring

Easy chocolate mousse *(6)* 🌾

In my first cookbook, I shared my best chocolate mousse recipe which is an elaborate and foolproof recipe that produces a superb dessert. Here, I offer a simplified version. Taking into consideration how easy this one is, the taste is surprisingly good!

250 grams or 1 cup heavy cream
250 grams or 8.5 ounces chocolate (good quality dark chocolate)
30 grams or 2 tablespoons rum or other liquor
25-50 grams or 2-4 tablespoons sugar (depending on how bitter you like your chocolate)
<u>**Topping**</u>
A pinch of sea salt flakes
Nuts of your choice, berries and/or zest of an orange

1. If you are serving children, warm up the rum in a small pot and set it on fire with a lighter so that the alcohol evaporates quickly. If you are not serving children, you may skip this step.
2. Place a pot with two cups of water over low heat and let it simmer. In a metal bowl, add the chocolate (cut into chunks) and place it over the simmering pot to melt the chocolate (Bain Marie, page 6). Alternatively, you can melt the chocolate in the microwave very carefully; cook it for 20-30 seconds, take it out to stir the chocolate, cook for another 20 seconds and stir again. Repeat the process, taking care that the chocolate does not burn until all is melted.
3. Place the heavy cream in a mixer bowl and start whisking at medium speed. As it begins to thicken (yogurt-like consistency) add the sugar, rum, and gradually the chocolate. When all the chocolate is incorporated and your cream has thickened, turn the mixer off. Transfer the mousse to a piping bag or use a spoon to divide it into six glasses (I estimate the serving size to be about 3 ounces). Sprinkle with orange zest or nuts and sea salt just before serving. Salt has the incredible capacity to enhance chocolate flavors, so do not skip it.

Ilse: You had made chocolate mousse for my birthday and I thought "this is the best birthday ever."
Emily: Nothing tops the chocolate mousse...nothing.

White Chocolate Mousse (12) 🌾

You can serve this mousse in small or medium glasses. It is fancy, tasty, very elegant, and very rich.

240 grams or 1 cup milk 3.5%
30 grams or 2 tablespoons dark rum
1/8 teaspoon salt
470 grams or 16.5 ounces white chocolate
2 gelatin sheets or 2 teaspoons of gelatin powder
240 grams or 1 cup cream

200 grams or 7 ounces raspberries fresh or frozen and a variety of berries

1. In a pot, warm up the milk with the rum and the salt just until it starts to steam. Turn the heat off and remove the milk from the heat before it starts to boil.
2. Cut the white chocolate into small chunks and place in a bowl. Pour the hot milk on the white chocolate and let it sit for two minutes for the chocolate to soften up. After two minutes mix slowly but thoroughly until all the chocolate melts.
3. If you are using gelatin sheets, soak them for five minutes in cold water. If you are using gelatin powder, add it to a cup with a small amount of water and let it absorb moisture for five minutes. Add the gelatin to the white chocolate mixture while still warm, and mix well with a whisk or a handheld blender until the gelatin is completely dissolved and not visible anymore (see page 6 for the instructions on gelatin use). Let the mixture cool down for 15-20 minutes,
4. In another bowl whisk up the cream until soft peaks form. Fold the cream in with the white chocolate mixture and transfer into a pitcher to facilitate serving the mousse.
5. Choose 12 small glasses. Place a few raspberries in each glass, divide the white chocolate mixture into the glasses, and top with a few more raspberries and /or other berries. Let it cool for a couple of hours in the fridge and serve.

Tip: Cream; Whenever cream is called for in this book, we mean heavy cream, 35% fat. Milk; Skim milk is never used in pastries. We normally use milk with 3.5% fat and, only if specified, 2%.

*"I can eat any amount you give me," said **Charlie,** before he got sick while hiking, after eating twenty-four (24) servings of white chocolate mousse.*

Almond Cake (8-12)

There are very few things I can say about this exquisite cake, except, please make it! When almond flavor is paired with a citrus aroma, the result is mouthwatering.

185 grams or 13 tablespoons unsalted butter (room temperature)
150 grams or 3/4 cup sugar
1 teaspoon pure vanilla extract
Zest of one orange
4 medium egg yolks
250 grams or 2 1/2 cups almond powder
130 grams or 1 cup flour
1 teaspoon baking powder
A pinch of salt
4 egg whites
50 grams or 1/4 cup sugar
A pinch of salt
Powdered sugar for decoration

1. Turn the oven to 380°F. In a mixing bowl place the butter (let it warm to room temperature or place in the microwave briefly), sugar, vanilla extract, and the zest of an orange (make sure that you have washed the orange with warm water to remove any protective wax first) and whisk at medium speed for 8-10 minutes until it becomes a fluffy, lighter in color mixture.
2. In the meantime mix the almond powder, flour, baking powder, and salt in another bowl.
3. Turn the mixer down to the slowest speed. Add egg yolks one by one and when incorporated add the flour mixture in batches. Be very careful so that the flour does not fly all over the kitchen. As soon as the flour mixture is incorporated, turn off the mixer. We do not want to overwork a cake batter after the flour is added. Extra mixing causes the gluten to develop and produces an elastic dough which is good for bread making but not for a cake batter. Make sure that no orange zest is left on the mixer whisk.
4. In another clean bowl beat the egg whites at medium speed. Once froth forms, start adding the sugar (1/4 cup) a tablespoon at a time and add a pinch of salt, too. A small amount of salt helps in stabilizing the meringue in addition to accentuating the flavors of our mixture. Turn the speed up to high and whip until you have a nice thick meringue.
5. With a rubber spatula start folding 1/3 of the meringue into the cake batter with slow and steady movements to lighten up the batter. Proceed with folding the rest of the meringue into the batter and mix until it is nicely incorporated. This cake batter is not going to be as runny as most cake batters are, but it is going to yield a very light cake because of the meringue. The taste of this cake, with the almond powder and the orange zest, is deep and delicate.
6. Transfer to a buttered cake form and bake for 50 to 55 minutes, depending on your oven, or until a knife comes out clean when inserted in the middle of the cake. Dust with powdered sugar.

Liann: *This cake tastes like a gift from the Greek gods-sent straight from Mt Olympus*

Tip: *Meringue (egg whites + sugar) is this magical component that will add wonderful fluffiness anywhere it is added. When a cake recipe starts by whisking sugar with butter, I like to proceed by adding the egg yolks first and then incorporating the egg whites in the form of meringue. Add a pinch of salt to your meringue; it helps stabilize the protein of the egg whites. The other, more common technique for cake batter, starts with whisking the eggs with the sugar thus creating an airy base to which you add the rest of the ingredients.*

Chocolate with Mandarin (24) 🍫 🌾

My dear friend Frieda is always baking something delicious. A few years ago she offered me some chocolate candy filled with mandarin peel. My mouth was flooded by waves of bitter chocolate and fresh citrus aroma. I was instantly hooked.

Peel of 8 medium mandarins (if you cut and press the peel it should fill up 1 cup)
100 grams or 1/2 cup sugar
30 grams or 2 tablespoons Cointreau or dark rum
40 grams or 1/3 cup blanched almonds
250 or 8 ounces of dark chocolate
A pinch of salt

1. Wash the mandarins in warm water and peel them. Remove the stem and any dark spots from the peels and cut them into chunks. We want to remove some of the bitterness of the peels but keep as much of the taste as possible. To do that we need to place them in two cups of cold water in a small pot and bring to a boil. Let it boil for three minutes (from the moment it starts to boil), drain, and add two more cups of cold water. Let it boil for another three minutes. Drain again, and repeat the process one more time. Three times in total.

2. After you drain the peels for the third time, place them in the pot with enough water to just cover them and add 1/2 cup sugar. You might need to add more water later, depending on the thickness of the peel of your mandarins. Bring to a very gentle simmer. Let them simmer for around 20 minutes until the peels start to turn translucent. Taste a small piece. It should be tender and very pleasant. We also want the water to have evaporated completely. If the peels are not tender yet, add water, a little at a time. When the peels are ready and the water is almost all gone add two tablespoons of Cointreau or rum, let this evaporate too, and turn the heat off. Let the peels cool completely.

3. In a heavy saucepan add the almonds and heat them for 4-5 minutes over medium heat to intensify the flavor and aroma. Let them cool slightly.

4. In a food processor add the peels and pulse for a few seconds at a time. Add the almonds and pulse again a couple of times. Do not overwork the mixture; we want to have some texture in the almonds. Form the mixture into small balls, cover them with plastic wrap and refrigerate them to let them set while you prepare the chocolate.

5. Melt the chocolate, temper it according to the instructions on page 7, and add a pinch of salt. Transfer the chocolate to a piping bag and pipe a few drops of chocolate into every socket of the chocolate mold. Turn the mold around to ensure that the sides of each socket are covered with chocolate. Turn upside down and tap over the chocolate bowl to get rid of the excess chocolate and ensure a uniform shell. Let the chocolate set in the refrigerator for a few minutes. Place one ball of the mandarin peels into every socket and then fill them with the rest of the chocolate. Tap the molds to ensure that no air bubbles are trapped and let the chocolate candies cool completely before you unmold them (please read instructions on using a chocolate mold on page 126). If you don't have a chocolate mold, place each mandarin ball on a fork and immerse it in the tempered chocolate. Take it out of the chocolate, tap a few times and place it on parchment paper to set. Proceed with the rest of the mandarin balls.

Daniel: *Fortunately, you don't have to go to China to eat these*

Tip: *Zest and peel of orange or lemon: Wash the fruit thoroughly with hot water, scrubbing the peel with a sponge to remove any protective wax.*

Mascarpone Tart with Red Fruit (8-12)

Crust
100 grams or 7 tablespoons cold unsalted butter
30 grams or 3 tablespoons powdered sugar
40 grams or 3 tablespoons sugar
1/2 teaspoon pure vanilla extract
1/4 teaspoon salt
1 egg divided into the yolk and egg white
150 grams or 1 cup plus 1 tablespoon flour
50 grams or 1/2 cup almond powder (or whole almonds that you process)

Filling
1 1/2 cup frozen red fruit (strawberries, blueberries, raspberries, or your choice)
25 grams or 2 tablespoons sugar
200 ml or 1 cup water
30 ml or 2 tablespoons cognac
4 sheets of gelatin or 4 teaspoons gelatin powder
300 grams or 1 1/4 cup heavy cream
310 grams or 1/1/4 cup mascarpone
25 grams or 3 tablespoons powdered sugar
1/4 teaspoon salt

1. In a food processor place the butter and the sugars along with the vanilla extract and the salt, and process until incorporated. Add the egg yolk, flour, and almond powder (almond flour is the same) and pulse briefly. Take a small amount of the dough in your palm and check if it holds together in a dough consistency. If it does not, add a tablespoon of icy water and pulse again. When the dough holds together, remove it from the food processor.

2. Preheat the oven to 380°F. Butter a 9-inch pie pan. Since there is almond powder in this dough, it will be difficult to roll. You can shape it by pushing it with your hands in the buttered pie pan. Make sure the thickness of the dough is the same all around, and the rim is cut straight. You can use a round pizza cutter to trim the top. Take time to create a smooth pie crust and then prick it with a fork several times. Take the pie shell to the oven and bake it for 25-30 minutes. When it is almost ready take it out of the oven and brush a little of the egg white (whisk it lightly first) onto the pie crust to seal the surface. Return the crust to the oven for 5 more minutes, until golden brown. Take it out of the oven and let it cool completely.

3. Place the gelatin in cold water according to the instructions on your package or on page 6.

4. Add the red fruit, the sugar, and the water to a small pot and bring to a boil. Add the cognac and immediately take the pot off the heat. Add the gelatin that you have already moistened into the red fruit mixture and stir until all the gelatin is dissolved.

5. Take 1/3 of the fruit mixture and puree it in a food processor. Proceed by adding the cream, mascarpone cheese, powdered sugar and salt, into the food processor with the pureed fruit and continue whisking until the mixture turns into a thick, beautiful pink cream. Add this cream to the pie crust and level the surface, making sure you cover the walls of the pie crust completely to isolate the crust. Let the cream cool and set slightly (15-20 min) and then carefully add the rest of the fruit mixture on the cream. Place the pie in the fridge until you serve.

Andrew: I would give up Dylan for this dessert.
Dylan: I would give up Andrew for this dessert.

Mille-Feuille *(16)*

Base
A package of puff pastry dough fresh or frozen (thawed)
Cream Patisserie
500 grams or 2 cups milk 3.5% fat
125 grams or 1/2 cup plus 2 tablespoons sugar
1/2 vanilla bean
2 whole eggs plus 1 egg yolk
30 grams or 4 tablespoons flour PLUS 20 grams or 3 tablespoons cornstarch
Topping
1/2 cup powdered sugar and fruit of your choice

1. Make the cream first: add the milk and the sugar to a pot. Do not stir the sugar as the sugar at the bottom of the pan acts as a protective layer that prevents the milk from burning. Cut a vanilla bean in half and then slice one half in the middle and scrape the seeds. Add the seeds and half a vanilla bean to the milk mixture. Save the rest of the vanilla bean by placing it in a jar with sugar. Turn the heat on medium-high and let the milk steam, but do not let it boil.

2. In a bowl whisk the eggs with the flour and the cornstarch thoroughly. When the milk starts to steam, add a ladle of the milk to the egg mixture with one hand while whisking the eggs with the other hand. Add a second and a third ladle of milk to the eggs in the bowl, and when half of the milk is added transfer the egg mixture to the pot, turn the heat on low, and vigorously stir for 20 seconds. Continue stirring until the cream starts to thicken.

3. As soon as the cream bubbles up, take it off the heat and transfer it to a clean bowl. Place it over an ice bath to stop the cooking and help the cream cool faster. In case the cream has curdled, whisk it with a handheld blender until the texture is smooth. Cover the cream with plastic wrap directly on its surface to prevent any skin from forming. Let the cream cool down and place it in the fridge for at least two hours.

4. Take the puff pastry sheets out of the fridge and place them on parchment paper on a cookie sheet. Place another piece of parchment paper on top and then a cookie sheet on top of the paper for weight, to keep the dough from puffing up too much. If you have a wire rack, use this on the dough; it works well as a weight on the puff pastry. Bake for 20 minutes at 360°F until golden brown. Take it out of the oven, remove the weight, flip the pastry sheets over and bake them for 10 more minutes to ensure thorough baking. Take them out of the oven and while still warm cut the pastry sheets into similar-size squares or rectangles.

5. When the phyllo pieces are completely cool take the cream out of the fridge. With a handheld mixer or blender, whisk the cream to regain its fluffiness (do not skip this step) for 3-4 minutes. Place the cream in a piping bag and pipe out a layer on a piece of the baked phyllo. Place another phyllo on top of the cream and pipe another layer. Add some crumbs of the phyllo and sprinkle some powdered sugar and cinnamon on top. Serve immediately with a few berries or the fruit of your choice. This dessert needs to be consumed within hours after assembling or the puff pastry will start to get soggy.

Alternatively, you may add the cream to pre-baked tartlet shells to create little elegant fruit tarts as seen in the picture. This is a great treat for a party.

Madison: *This dessert is delicious, perfectly fulfilling, yet light and airy at the same time.*

Tip: *We mostly use vanilla extract because vanilla beans are expensive. However, some desserts, like this pastry cream, do require the use of a vanilla bean. Use half a bean for 12-16 people and store the other half in the sugar jar. The bean will be kept moist and the sugar will be infused with the wonderful vanilla scent. In general, when using a vanilla bean, add it as early as possible to infuse flavor.*

French brownies (12-16) 🌾

Every good cookbook has a few star recipes. When you make them they become an instant favorite. This recipe is one of the star recipes in this cookbook! Please try it!

200 grams or 7 ounces dark chocolate
120 grams or 1 stick unsalted butter

4 eggs
125 grams or 1 cup plus 2 tablespoons sugar

75 grams or 3/4 cup almond powder
1 teaspoon of pure vanilla extract
A generous pinch of sea salt flakes

1. Preheat the oven to 340°F. Melt the chocolate with the butter in a Bain Marie (page 6) and mix until well incorporated.
2. Whisk the eggs and the sugar with a hand mixer, or in a mixer bowl, until the mixture has doubled in volume, is lighter in color and has reached a ribbon consistency. (When you lift the whisk, the batter that drops from the whisk creates a thread that stays on the batter's surface and is visible for a few seconds. This is called ribbon consistency.)
3. You may use blanched or unblanched almonds. Place them in the food processor and grind them to a fine sand texture or buy ready almond powder or flour (same). Add the melted chocolate and butter, almond powder, and vanilla to the beaten egg mixture. Mix thoroughly with a spatula.
4. Transfer the mixture to a baking dish (you don't even need to butter it) that is 9x9 square or round, 8 or 9 inches in diameter. Sprinkle the top with a pinch of sea salt, crushing any big flakes with your fingers, and bake. In about 35-40 minutes a crust will have formed. You can either take it out then, and it will be very moist inside, or you can bake it for another ten minutes, depending on how you like your brownies.

These brownies are even better the next day. *IF* there is a next day…

The brownie in this picture is baked for 40 minutes.

Alexander: *Turns out, if you make them for your pregnant wife, she will love you forever.*
Morgan: *BEST BROWNIES I HAVE EVER HAD. Period.*

Charlotte (8-12)

You need a candy thermometer to make this impressive dessert. It is a good excuse to get one. This recipe yields 8 cups of dessert (ladyfingers and all), so choose your mold accordingly.

1 package of ladyfingers (8 ounces)
<u>**Syrup for Ladyfingers**</u>
250 grams or 1 1/4 cup water
150 grams or 3/4 cup sugar
8 grams or 1 tablespoon cocoa
40 grams or 3 tablespoons dark rum
<u>**Italian Meringue**</u>
2 egg whites (room temperature)
125 grams or 1/2 cup and 2 tablespoons sugar
25 grams or 2 tablespoons water
<u>**Ganache**</u>
300 grams or 1 1/4 cup heavy cream
300 grams or 10 ounces dark chocolate
(plus another 150 grams or 5 oz for decoration)
A generous pinch of salt
1 teaspoon pure vanilla extract

1. Make the syrup for the ladyfingers by adding the water, sugar, and cocoa to a pot. Bring to a boil and stir. Add the rum and turn the heat off immediately. Let the syrup cool down.

2. In a small pot add the sugar and water for the Italian meringue and mix to dissolve. It is important to clean the walls of the pot with a wet brush before you turn the heat on, to avoid crystallization (page 8). Place the candy thermometer in and turn the heat on at medium-high.

3. In a mixer bowl add the egg whites. Turn the mixer on at medium speed.

4. This is the most technical step and you need to be precise. Once the syrup/caramel in the small pot reaches 250°F (it will be white and starting to turn yellow around the edge, take it off the heat *before* it starts to get brown) turn the mixer with the egg whites on high and immediately take the syrup off the heat and slowly start adding it to the egg whites (by now they should be fluffy) very slowly in a very thin flow, like a thread. Once you add all the syrup, turn the mixer speed down to medium again and let it whisk for ten more minutes until the meringue cools down to lukewarm. This is the Italian meringue.

5. In a pot, heat the cream. Chop the chocolate (300 gr or 10 oz) and place it in a bowl along with the salt and vanilla. Once the cream steams up, add it to the chocolate. Wait for 3 minutes for the chocolate to soften and slowly start stirring until your mixture (ganache) is smooth. Let it cool slightly.

6. Fold the Italian meringue into the ganache with a spatula until fully incorporated.

7. Find a bowl with tall sides, straight or conical in shape (the top is wider than the bottom). Take the ladyfingers and one by one immerse in the cool syrup for 3-4 seconds. Line them at the bottom and around the sides of the bowl. Transfer half of the chocolate mixture to the dish, and add a layer of moistened ladyfingers on the chocolate. Add the rest of the chocolate

and finish with another layer of ladyfingers. Cover and leave in the fridge for at least 4 hours. To unmold, place the dish in warm water briefly, and then turn it upside down on a platter.

8. In a Bain Marie melt the chocolate for decoration (150 gr) and pour it into a bowl lined with plastic wrap or bubble wrap. Let the chocolate cool completely and unmold by peeling the plastic or bubble wrap off the chocolate carefully. You will have a chocolate bowl that you can fill with the fruit of your choice. Strawberries, raspberries, and oranges work very well.

Casey: I like this char-LOT-te!

Apple Cake with Cream (12-16)

What is unique about this cake is that we make a pastry cream and pipe it out on top of the cake batter. Baking the cake with this cream produces a wonderful top and a juicy cake.

Cream

50 grams or 1/4 cup sugar
16 grams or 2 tablespoons flour
1/2 teaspoon pure vanilla extract
240 grams or 1 cup milk
1 egg

Cake

3 eggs
300 grams or 1 1/2 cup sugar
1 teaspoon pure vanilla extract
180 grams or 1 1/2 stick butter (room temperature)
390 grams or 3 cups flour
1 tablespoon baking powder
1/8 teaspoon salt
1 tablespoon cinnamon
1/4 teaspoon ground cloves
230 grams or 1 cup whole milk

3 medium apples
Powdered sugar for decoration

1. In a small pot add the sugar and flour and mix thoroughly. Add the vanilla, cold milk, and egg and whisk very well. Turn the heat on low and start stirring constantly until the mixture bubbles up. Take it off the heat immediately and transfer it to a clean bowl through a sieve to catch any flour lumps. Cover with plastic wrap directly on the surface and let the cream cool down. In about 15 minutes transfer the cream to a piping bag,

2. In the mixer bowl add the eggs, sugar, and vanilla extract and whisk until lighter in color. Add the soft butter, cut into small pieces, and continue whisking until the mixture is smooth.

3. In another bowl add the flour, baking powder, salt, cinnamon, cloves, and mix. Turn the mixer off and fold 1/3 of the flour mixture and half the milk into the batter. Add another 1/3 of the flour and the rest of the milk and fold again. Finish by folding in the rest of the flour.

4. Turn the oven to 380°F and butter a springform cake pan. You may use a regular 9 or 10-inch diameter form or a 7-inch diameter form, which will result in a taller cake. In this case, you will need to bake the cake for an additional 10-15 minutes.

5. Peel the apples and slice them with a mandoline so that the pieces have the same thickness, about 1/8 of an inch. Place a ladle of the batter in the form, layer apple slices, and then add another ladle of the batter. Arrange a second layer of apples and continue until you finish with layering, alternating the apples and the batter. Pipe the cream on top either in a swirl motif or by crossing lines. Save the rest of the cream in the fridge. Place the cake in the oven and bake for 55-60 minutes (or 78-80 if your cake is taller). Let the cake cool completely and unmold. Sprinkle with powdered sugar and serve with the rest of the cream.

Mike: Best apple cake I've ever had. NO, best dessert I've ever had.

Red velvet cake (12-16)

Red velvet cake is a Southern United States dessert. I do not pretend to be an expert in Southern United States desserts, but I could not pass up the opportunity to sneak in some healthy vegetables in a wonderful dessert…

2 medium beetroots or 1 big one (about 120 grams or 4 ounces)
50 grams or 1/4 cup sugar
1 tablespoon cornstarch
150 grams or 3/4 cup sugar
200 grams or 14 tablespoons butter (room temperature)
4 eggs
130 grams or 3/4 cup dark or semisweet chocolate chips
160 grams or 1 cup plus 2 tablespoons flour
1 tablespoon baking powder
1/8 teaspoon salt
8 grams or 1 tablespoon cocoa
Topping 1 (pictured here)
250 grams or 1 cup cream cheese or mascarpone cheese
250 grams or 2 cups powdered sugar
Topping 2 (my favorite)
5 tablespoons Tahini sauce
3 tablespoons honey
1 teaspoon cinnamon
1 tablespoon cognac (if you are not serving children)

1. Peel the beetroot with a potato peeler and cut it into small pieces so that the food processor will process it easier. Process it until it resembles coarse sand. Place the beet with 1/4 cup sugar and 1/2 cup water in a small pot and cook until almost all the water has evaporated, about 5 minutes. Just before all the water is gone, add the cornstarch dissolved in 1/4 cup water. Stir it up until it starts to boil and then turn the heat off. Let the beet mixture cool down. I like to save a teaspoon of the juice of this mixture for coloring the icing.

2. Turn the oven on to 380°F. Butter a bundt cake form and lightly dust it with flour.

3. In a mixer bowl, add the rest of the sugar (3/4 cup) and the butter and whisk at medium speed until it is lighter in color. Add the eggs, one at a time, and continue whisking. Turn the mixer off and fold in the beet mixture and the chocolate chips. In another bowl mix the flour, baking powder, salt, and cocoa and incorporate the flour mixture into the cake batter.

4. Transfer the cake batter into the form and place it in the oven. Bake for 50-55 minutes.

5. If you are using Topping 1, add all ingredients plus a teaspoon of the beet mixture juice to a bowl and whisk until all are incorporated. Drizzle over the cake after it has cooled down.

If you are using Topping 2 (which is a very Greek, very healthy, and tasty alternative) mix the ingredients by hand. They will thicken up very quickly to a thick paste. Place it in a bowl so that your guests can help themselves to the topping. This is an appealing topping on a very interesting cake. Our students love it and I think you will enjoy it, too.

Robin: *This cake BEET all other cakes. Seriously, this is the best Red Velvet cake I have ever had and red velvet is my grandma's specialty. (Please don't tell her).*

Red velvet with strawberries (12)

This recipe with strawberries is a variation of the red velvet cake in case beetroot is too extreme for you. The color of the cake with strawberries is not going to be as intense but it is not worth adding artificial coloring which truly is not good for you.

100-120 grams or 1 cup fresh or frozen strawberries
100 grams or 1/2 cup sugar
2 tablespoons cornstarch

150 grams or 3/4 cup sugar
200 grams or 14 tablespoons butter (room temperature)
4 eggs
180 grams or 1 1/4 cup flour
2 tablespoons baking powder
8 grams or 1 tablespoon cocoa
A pinch of salt
<u>Mascarpone Icing</u>
240 grams or 1 cup heavy cream
230 grams or 1 cup mascarpone or cream cheese
20 grams or 2 tablespoons powdered sugar
12 fresh strawberries for decoration (or 18 if using small cupcakes)
100 grams or 4 ounces dark chocolate

1. With a handheld blender, puree the strawberries and transfer them to a small pot along with 1/2 cup sugar. Turn the heat on low and cook for 5 minutes. Dissolve the cornstarch in three tablespoons of cold water and add to the strawberries. Cook until the mixture thickens up about one more minute and then take it off the heat. Set aside to cool.

2. Turn the oven on to 360°F. Line a muffin pan with 12 big paper cups or 18 medium ones.

3. In a mixer bowl, add the sugar and butter and whisk at medium speed until it is lighter in color. Add the eggs, one at a time, and continue whisking. In another bowl, mix the flour, baking powder, cocoa, and salt. Turn the mixer down to the slowest speed and incorporate the flour mixture. Turn the mixer off as soon as the flour is incorporated.

4. Add the strawberry mixture to the cake batter. Fold in carefully and divide into the paper cups. Bake the cupcakes for 20-25 minutes, check for doneness and let them cool completely.

5. In a mixer bowl, add the cream and the mascarpone (or cream cheese) with the powdered sugar. Whip until it thickens up. Transfer to a piping bag and decorate the cupcakes with it. Melt the chocolate in a bain-marie and temper it (see page 7). Dip the fresh strawberries (after you have washed and dried them) into the melted chocolate, let the chocolate set and decorate the strawberry muffins with them.

These cupcakes make an excellent garden party treat!

Ashley: The best snack after our pool party.

Oreo cupcakes (12-16)

1 package of original OREOS (you will use 6 ounces)
100 grams or 4 ounces dark chocolate finely chopped or baker's chocolate chips
100 grams or 1/2 cup sugar
4 eggs
1 teaspoon pure vanilla extract
1/4 teaspoon salt
200 grams or 14 tablespoons butter (room temperature, very soft)
100 grams or 3/4 cup flour
1 tablespoon baking powder

240 grams or 1 cup heavy cream
8 grams or 1 tablespoon cocoa
30 grams or 3 tablespoons powdered sugar

1. Take twelve cookies and open them up. You will end up with twenty-four single cookies. Some of them will have more cream than others. Place the twelve with the least cream in the bottom of the cupcake paper holders, cream side facing up. Don't worry if some break. Place the cookies, with the most cream on them, into the food processor along with 100 grams of chocolate finely chopped. Pulse a couple of times, very briefly.

2. Turn the oven to 360°F.

3. In a mixer, beat the sugar and the eggs for 7-8 minutes at medium speed until you achieve ribbon consistency. Continue whisking and add the vanilla extract and salt, along with the soft butter. Whisk until all ingredients are incorporated. Turn the mixer off.

4. Place the flour and baking powder in a bowl along with the chocolate-OREO mixture and mix. Fold the flour mixture into the cake batter, carefully. Transfer it to a piping bag without a nozzle to facilitate you in dividing the batter.

5. Take the paper cupcake molds (that already have half an OREO at the bottom) and place them in a muffin or cupcake pan. Fill up the paper cupcake molds 3/4 of the way with the cake batter, with the help of the piping bag, and bake for 20 minutes.

6. Beat the heavy cream with 3 tablespoons powdered sugar until thick. Transfer to a piping bag, this time with a round or a star nozzle.

7. Because the muffins have chocolate chunks or chips, they are irresistible when they are still warm and the chocolate is melted. When (or should we say *if*) the cupcakes cool down completely, decorate with the whipped cream, dust with cocoa powder and add the rest of the OREO cookies, whole or in chunks.

Tip: Butter is one of the most important ingredients in pastry making because the quality and taste of butter are determining factors in the dessert. Pastry chefs choose a brand and never deviate from it because the taste of the specific butter gives a distinct flavor to their desserts. Follow each recipe carefully, using cold or room-temperature butter as specified. In this cookbook whenever butter is mentioned, we mean European-style unsalted butter.

Berkley: *A million times better than any OREO dessert I have ever tried.*
Emma: *I had a dream last night. I dreamed that we had the Oreo cupcakes with lemon yogurt ...*

(recipe of Lemon Yogurt on page 186)

Carrot cake Cupcakes (12-16)

There is something irresistible about a good carrot cake. I am not sure if it is the cinnamon aroma or the unconscious knowledge that you are eating a ton of carrots—thus a healthy dessert—but it is very hard to resist a good, aromatic carrot cake.

220 grams or 2 cups grated carrots (about five big carrots)
400 grams or 2 cups sugar —I like to use 1 cup white, and 1 cup brown sugar
4 eggs
260 grams or 2 cups flour
1/2 teaspoon baking soda
1 teaspoon baking powder
1/4 teaspoon salt
2 tablespoons cinnamon
170 grams or 1 cup vegetable oil
Buttercream OR you can use Mascarpone icing (page 30)
960 grams or 4 cups milk
1/2 vanilla bean or 1 teaspoon pure vanilla extract
8 egg yolks
300 grams or 1 1/2 cup sugar
85 grams or 12 tablespoons cornstarch (be very precise in leveling the spoon)
A pinch of salt
360 grams or 3 sticks butter (you may use only 2 sticks if you wish)

1. Wash and peel the carrots. Cut them in chunks and grate them in a food processor. Measure 2 cups by pressing them in the cupholder lightly. Set them aside and turn the oven to 360°F.

2. In a bowl, place the sugar and eggs and start whisking at medium speed until they double in volume and become lighter in color, about 8-10 minutes. Turn the mixer off.

3. Add the baking soda and baking powder, salt and cinnamon to the flour and mix. Fold half of the flour into the batter carefully before adding the oil; stir, and add the rest of the flour and fold. Add the carrots and mix until all are incorporated. Divide the mixture into the cupcake holders and bake for 20-25 minutes.

4. In a pan with a heavy bottom, warm the milk and the half vanilla bean or vanilla extract. In another bowl, add the egg yolks, sugar, cornstarch and salt and mix very well. When the milk starts to steam, take one ladle of the milk and add it to the egg mixture. Mix well. Take a second ladle and mix, and then a third. Transfer the egg mixture to the pan of milk (over very low heat) and stir vigorously for 20 sec. Continue stirring until the mixture bubbles. Take it off the heat immediately and transfer it into a mixer bowl. Turn the mixer on at the lowest speed and whisk while the cream cools down (5-8 min). When the cream feels warm (around 110°F), cut the butter into small cubes and start adding them to the cream. When all the butter is incorporated, turn the mixer off. Transfer the buttercream to a piping bag and let it cool completely to set. When cool, pipe onto your carrot cake cupcakes.

I made decorative carrots out of marzipan (almond paste) using a little orange and green food coloring, and I also used some chocolate soil for decoration (see page 70, step 5).

Emily: *I have yet to find a carrot cake that tops Natasa's!*

Blueberry muffins (12)

80 grams or 1/2 cup vegetable oil
200 grams or 1 cup sugar
1 teaspoon pure vanilla extract
Zest of one lemon
2 eggs
100 grams or 1 cup oat flour
(oats grated to a fine powder)
70 grams or 1/2 cup all-purpose flour
(look at step 3)
50 grams or 1/2 cup almond flour
2 teaspoons baking powder
A pinch of salt
100 grams or 1/2 cup yogurt
10 grams or 1 tablespoon powdered sugar
150 grams or 1 cup fresh blueberries
25 grams or 2 tablespoons sugar

1. Preheat the oven to 420°F. Prepare 12 muffin molds by placing paper cups in them or buttering them.

2. In a mixer bowl combine the vegetable oil along with the sugar, vanilla, and lemon zest and turn the speed to medium. Add the eggs one by one and whisk for four or five more minutes. Turn the mixer off.

3. Combine the three flours with the baking powder and salt and mix well. If there is a nut allergy or a gluten allergy, skip the almond or regular flour, respectively, and increase the oat flour by the same amount. The total amount of flour you use should be two cups (around 220 grams). The muffins will be crumbly if you skip the regular flour altogether, but just, if not more, tasty.

4. Fold half the flour mixture into the egg mixture and add the yogurt. Combine and then add the rest of the flour and mix just until all ingredients are incorporated.

5. Save a few blueberries for decoration. Mix the rest of the blueberries with a tablespoon of powdered sugar to coat them and add them to the batter. Fold carefully and divide the mixture into the muffin molds. Sprinkle with a little sugar and place into the oven.

6. Five minutes later lower the heat to 370°F and bake for another 18-20 minutes. Take the muffins out of the oven and let them cool completely. Decorate with the rest of the blueberries and lemon zest.

Julie: *There is just MUFFIN better than this!*

Baba au Rum or Savarin with Rum *(12)*

In Babette's Feast, a 1987 Danish film that won the Oscar for Best Foreign Language Movie, Babette prepares an incredible meal for the people who saved her life. She serves Baba au Rum for dessert. A truly unforgettable treat!

8 grams or 1 envelope of dry yeast
80 grams or 1/3 cup lukewarm milk
25 grams or 2 tablespoons sugar
2 eggs (room temperature)
1 egg yolk
250 grams or 2 cups bread flour (12-14% protein)
90 grams or 6 tablespoons butter (soft, not melted)
<u>**Syrup**</u>
400 grams or 2 cups water
250 grams or 1 1/4 cup sugar
50 grams or 4 tablespoons rum
Peel strips of one lemon and one orange
<u>**Topping**</u>
5 tablespoons apricot or orange marmalade
250 grams or 1 cup heavy cream
2 cups strawberries or fruit of your choice

1. Warm up the milk slightly (110°F). In the mixer bowl, add the milk, yeast and 2 TB of sugar. Turn the mixer on low, using the kneading hook. Add the eggs and the egg yolk and then gradually incorporate the flour. Let the mixer work the dough for 7-8 minutes. It is extremely important to use bread flour (12-14% protein) for this cake so that the protein in the flour forms strong gluten ties and creates the characteristic big air holes we see in bread. These holes will then absorb our syrup which will result in this magnificent dessert.

2. Gradually add the butter (warm it up slightly; it should be soft but NOT melted). Keep kneading for 5 more minutes until the dough is smooth and shiny. Turn the mixer off, cover it with a towel, and let the dough double in volume. It will be sticky. Do not add more flour.

3. Butter a bundt form and sprinkle it with flour, or use small individual ramekins. Butter them and lightly flour each one. Pinch the risen dough down and transfer it to the bundt cake, spreading it as evenly as possible. Let it rise again.

4. Turn the oven to 380°F. Very carefully transfer the bundt form to the oven and bake for 45-50 minutes (30-35 if individual ramekins are used) until a deep golden brown surface is achieved. Unmold the Savarin (this is the name of this dough) to a platter and let it cool.

5. In a small pot, boil the syrup ingredients. Transfer the cake back to the bundt mold (to help it keep its form) and prick it several times with a fork. Slowly and carefully drench the cool cake with the boiling syrup. Use all the syrup, even if it looks too much. Now, you have to let the cake absorb the syrup for at least two hours or preferably overnight in the fridge.

6. Unmold the cake on a platter. Warm up the marmalade (you may add a tablespoon of rum if you wish) and with a brush apply it to the cake. Whip the cream in a mixer until soft peaks are formed and transfer it to a piping bag. Decorate with whipped cream and fruit.

Tip: With baking powder, we use all-purpose flour that creates a soft and crumbly product (cakes, cookies). But in desserts that contain yeast, it is imperative that we use strong flour, as we do in bread and pizza dough. Strong flour contains a higher percentage of protein (12-14%), which results in stronger gluten development. Gluten creates strong connections that can hold the rising dough, thus creating a spongy and elastic texture, with big air holes, very characteristic of yeast dough.

Gâteau de Voyage: There is a category of French cakes called "Desserts for Traveling", Gâteau de Voyage. They were made in an era when traveling by horse took time so you needed to carry a dessert that kept fresh for many days. One common characteristic of these desserts is a glaze that seals the cake, keeping it moist and fresh for days without it being refrigerated. Another very common element is honey, which is a natural antibacterial, preserving anything that comes in contact with it. The following three cakes are Gateau de Voyage. This one is my absolute favorite cake.

Pistachio Cake (8-12)

Note: Almonds can be substituted for pistachios

When my son was a student in the US he would take a block of this cake back with him every time he came home. He ate a small bit every morning with coffee and it lasted for more than a month, without ever refrigerating it.

180 grams or 1 1/2 stick butter
330 grams or 2 2/3 cups powdered sugar
120 grams or 1 cup pistachios finely ground
200 grams or 1 1/2 cup flour
2 teaspoons baking powder
1/8 teaspoon salt
1 teaspoon pure vanilla extract
30 grams or 1 1/2 tablespoons honey
45 grams or 3 tablespoons dark rum
240 grams or 7 egg whites

Royal Icing: 1 egg white + 1.5 cups of powdered sugar + a handful of chopped pistachios
Optional Raspberry Coulis: 3 tablespoon water +1/2 cup sugar + 10 ounces raspberries

1. Turn the oven to 380°F.
2. Place the butter in a small pot over medium heat. Let it melt and keep it over the heat until foam starts to form on the surface. As soon as the color of the butter turns golden brown (you will see dark particles at the bottom and it will start to smell nutty) take the butter off the heat and let it cool. You now have beurre noisette, which French cuisine uses to add deep flavor.
3. Mix all the dry ingredients and then add the honey, rum, and egg whites. (I keep the egg yolks in a jar in the fridge and use them to make Tiramisu or a lemon tart). Mix thoroughly.
4. After the butter has cooled down slightly add it to the batter through a sieve to catch all the burned particles which you discard. Mix well.
5. Butter a 9x12 pan or a round 10-inch spring pan and add the batter. Bake for 50-55 minutes until an inserted knife comes out clean. Let the cake cool slightly before you unmold it.
6. You may use meringue powder or an egg white, or if you are uncomfortable with a regular egg white, a pasteurized egg white to make a thin royal icing. Whisk it up with one cup of powdered sugar. Keep adding a tablespoon of sugar while you whisk the icing until you reach a thin royal icing consistency. Depending on the heat, the humidity, and the freshness of the

egg, it usually takes 1 1/2 cups of sugar. Spread over the cool cake and the sides until it is completely covered so that the cake does not dry out. Decorate with chopped pistachios. The taste of this dessert keeps getting deeper and better as the days go by. Do not refrigerate it.

<u>Raspberry Coulis</u>; You may serve this with the cake. In a pot add the water and sugar and bring to a boil. Add the raspberries and boil for five minutes. Puree the sauce with a handheld blender and pass it through a sieve to remove the seeds. Serve cold.

Shannon: I made sure I was first in line for dessert that day! SO good!
Ryan: This pistachio cake is so flavorful with great texture!

Orange Travel Cake (12-16)

180 grams or 1 1/2 sticks unsalted butter
5 eggs
220 grams or 1 cup plus 1 tablespoon sugar
30 grams or 3 tablespoons orange juice
Zest of 3 oranges
10 grams or 1 tablespoon lemon juice
Zest of 1 lemon
1/4 teaspoon salt
60 grams or 3 tablespoons honey
300 grams or 2 1/4 cup flour
8 grams or 2 teaspoons baking powder
120 grams or 1/2 cup cream

Glaze 1. 1/2 cup orange marmalade and 1 tablespoon cognac (optional)
Glaze 2. <u>Mirror glaze:</u> 1 cup sweetened condensed milk, 200 grams or 7 oz white chocolate, 2 gelatin sheets, and a pinch of salt. Optionally a drop of food coloring.

1. Place the butter in a small pot over medium-high heat. Let it melt and be attentive while you let it on the stove for a few more minutes, as the butter starts to burn slightly. Take it off the heat as soon as a wonderful nutty smell fills the kitchen and golden brown color is achieved. You will see burned particles sinking at the bottom of the pan. Set it aside to cool.
2. Turn the oven to 400°F. Butter a big bundt cake pan (9 or 10 inches) and lightly flour it.
3. In a mixer bowl add the eggs and sugar and whisk at medium-high speed for 7-8 minutes until they double their volume.
4, Turn the mixer to low and add the juices, zest, salt, and honey.
5. Turn the mixer off, and fold in half the flour with the baking powder. Add the cream and then the rest of the flour, and fold with a spatula until all the flour is incorporated.
6. Add the cooled butter through a sieve to catch the burned particles which you discard.
7. Transfer the batter to the bundt pan and bake for 50-55 minutes until a knife comes out clean when inserted into the cake.
8. When the cake is cool, unmold it on a platter. **Glaze 1.** Warm up the Orange marmalade together with a teaspoon of cognac or water and apply with a brush to the cake. Brush on 2-3 layers to create a thick and luscious covering that will keep the cake fresh for days.
Glaze 2. Place a bowl over a bain-marie (page 6) and add the sweetened condensed milk. In a small bowl with water add the gelatin (sheet or powder) to moisten it according to the instructions on page 6. Cut the white chocolate into small pieces. When the condensed milk/marmalade mixture gets warm (120-130°F) add the white chocolate pieces. Mix over the bain-marie, until all chocolate melts. Take the bowl off the bain-marie and continue mixing for 1 minute. Add the gelatin and mix until all is incorporated. If you want to add food coloring, add it now. When the mixture cools down slightly and reaches 110°F (lukewarm), pour over the cake and let it set. It is a very tasty and beautiful glaze.

Anna: *That white chocolate frosting!!! On that tangy cake! Delicious!*

Financier (16)

200 grams or 14 tablespoons of butter
4 egg whites
200 grams or 1 cup sugar
65 grams or 1/2 cup flour
110 grams or 1 cup plus 2 tablespoons almond powder (almond flour is the same)
A pinch of salt
4 tablespoons fresh orange juice
Zest of one orange

1/2 cup apricot or orange marmalade
1 tablespoon rum (optional)

1. Place the butter in a pot over medium heat. Let the butter melt and cook until it starts to turn golden brown. Do not leave it unattended because it can burn very quickly. Take it off the heat as soon as you can see burned particles and a nutty and very pleasant aroma wafts all around. Set it aside to cool.
2. Turn the oven to 360°F. Carefully and generously butter a financier silicone tray. The financier molds have small rectangular shapes. If you don't have a financier mold tray, use any small molds you have. The silicon ones will unmold easier than the tin ones.
3. In a mixer bowl add the egg whites and start whisking. Slowly add the sugar. Turn the mixer off as soon as a nice thick meringue is formed. (If you turn the bowl upside down the meringue should not move.)
4. With a spatula fold the flour, almond flour, and salt into the meringue. Add the orange juice and zest and fold carefully. Through a sieve (to catch the brown burned protein particles) add the butter once it has cooled to lukewarm. Fold the batter until completely incorporated.
5. For an easier way to fill the financier molds I use a piping bag. Fill it up with the cake batter or use a spoon to divide the batter into the financier molds, filling them 3/4 of the way. Place in the oven and bake for 20-22 minutes or until a nice golden crust is created.
6. Take them out of the oven, unmold on a platter, and let them cool slightly. In a small pot warm up the apricot or orange marmalade with a tablespoon of rum or water. Brush the financiers twice and let them absorb the jam. Sprinkle with orange zest or place a stick of candied orange peel on every financier and serve with hot tea. They are small, elegant and very, very tasty.

Dylan: *This is triple-decker bussin*

Madeleine (48)

Madeleines are famous French tiny cakes with a very sweet history of origin. Madeleines were originally made in seashells, but you may use molds now! Many things have to be right when you make Madeleines: they have to be moist inside, they have to be darker on the bottom and above all, they have to have a hump! They are delicious and very elegant!

200 grams or 14 tablespoons butter
4 eggs
200 grams or 1 cup sugar
20 grams or 1 tablespoon honey
1 teaspoon pure vanilla extract
200 grams or 1 1/2 cups flour
2 teaspoons baking powder
A pinch of salt
Flavoring: 4 tablespoons lemon juice and zest of 1 lemon OR 6 tablespoons orange juice and zest of 2 oranges OR 1/4 cup grated pistachio OR 4 tablespoons lavender water*

1. In a small pot start melting the butter. As soon as half of it is melted, take it off the heat and stir it for a minute until it is in between solid and liquid. It should be like a thick cream. The butter consistency is very important for the success of the Madeleines. Set it aside.

2. In a mixer bowl add the eggs and sugar and whisk for 8-10 minutes. Turn the mixer to low and add the honey and vanilla extract. Add chosen flavoring. You may divide your batter in half and use two different flavorings, in which case you need to add half the amount of the flavoring indicated here since you are using half the batter for it.

3. Turn the mixer off, add the butter and incorporate it very well. Fold in the flour with the baking powder and salt. If you are using grated pistachios you need to use 1/4 cup less flour.

4. Cover the batter with plastic wrap directly on the surface and place it in the fridge for at least six hours or better overnight (or up to 2 days). If you are using more than one flavor, you may divide the batter into glass containers with lids.

5. When you are ready to bake them, turn the oven to 425°F. Butter the molds. Fill a piping bag with the (cold and thick) batter and pipe it into the mold 3/4 of the way. If you do not have Madeleine molds you may use any small mold you have, even muffin pans. Place the filled molds in the fridge until the oven heats up well. We want to create a thermal shock, so the colder the batter is, the better.

6. Place the mold in the oven on the lower rack and bake for 6 minutes. Lower the heat to 355°F and bake for another 6 to 9 minutes. Take the Madeleines out of the oven and unmold them immediately to cool. Madeleines are consumed the same day, preferably warm.

Note: If you are not consuming them the same day, cover them with a light frosting to keep them moist: let them cool completely and then whisk one egg white with 1 1/2 cup powdered sugar. Color the icing slightly, with a color that matches your flavoring. Dip the Madeleines in it. Let them dry and decorate with lemon zest, orange zest, or the topping of your choice.

*If you are making lavender Madeleines, place 4 lavender flowers in half a cup of water. Bring to a boil, turn the heat off, cover the pot and let the water infuse with the flavor for 20 minutes. Add 4 tablespoons of the water to the batter in Step 2.

Asparagus Tart (8)

1/2 package of phyllo dough (you could use another dough if you prefer)
3 tablespoons olive oil or butter

10 ounces spring slender asparagus
2 tablespoons salt
80 grams or 1 cup grated mozzarella or Emmental cheese
120 grams or 1/2 cup heavy cream
200 grams or 1 cup Greek yogurt
2 eggs
1/2 teaspoon salt
Fresh pepper
Fresh nutmeg

1. Wash the asparagus and snap off the bottom inch of the stalk. Asparagus should snap at the right point where the edible part is separated from the woody part of the stalk that is too fibrous to eat. (The part of the asparagus stalk that is inedible can be boiled. It will give you a tasteful broth that can be used in soups or sauces).

2. In a large pot bring 3 cups of water to a boil. Add two tablespoons of salt and the asparagus. Let the asparagus boil for 4 minutes. Remove asparagus from boiling water and immediately immerse them in ice water to halt the cooking. One minute later take them out and place them on a kitchen towel to dry.

3. Turn the oven to 400°F.

4. Butter a pie pan and open your phyllo dough package. Apply melted butter or olive oil on the first phyllo and lay it on the pie shell, butter side up. With your fingers create a pleated layer so that the rectangular phyllo becomes a square. We do this so that the pleats and the air pockets that are formed will create crunchiness and fluffiness. Butter another phyllo and transfer it on top of the first, again creating pleats, but this time taking care that the pleats of the second phyllo are perpendicular to the first ones. Now spread two tablespoons of the cheese on the second phyllo to create a crunchy and delicious layer. Butter two or three more phyllos and repear the process creating five or six layers in total.

5. Sprinkle the rest of the cheese on top of the last phyllo.

6. Take the asparagus and cut each in half. Reserve the top beautiful halves intact but chop the bottom stalks into half-inch pieces.

7. Beat eggs with the cream and yogurt until smooth. Add salt and pepper and then the chopped asparagus pieces. Transfer the mixture to the pie crust on top of the cheese. Decorate with the beautiful asparagus tops placing them in a circular mode with half of them looking towards the center of the pie and half looking the other way. Sprinkle with pepper and grate fresh nutmeg on the filling. Turn the overhanging phyllo inward over the filling. Apply the rest of the butter or oil to the overlaying phyllo and place the pie in the oven. Bake for 45 minutes or until the pie gets a beautiful deep golden color and the filling is set. Serve warm.

Summer

Fruit Salad in Ice Bowl with Sabayon

A few years ago serving fruit salad in ice bowls decorated with small flowers at garden parties was very fashionable in Greece. It is simply stunning, and I hope you give it a try.

Take two bowls, preferably metal ones. One must be noticeably bigger than the other. Place the smaller in the bigger one and attach their tops with duct tape so that a ring of empty space is created between the two rims. Try to tape them in a way that the ring has the same thickness all around.

In a big pot add a quart of water, bring it to a boil and let the water cool completely. Ice made with boiled water is translucent and will produce a beautiful ice bowl. Fill the in-between space of the taped bowls with the water you boiled, which is now at room temperature. If the water is still warm the flowers will discolor. Place small flowers with their leaves in the water and take the two bowls to the freezer. I also add some red berries. One hour later, take the bowls out of the freezer and with a fork, try to push down and reposition the flowers. The flowers usually move as you place the bowls in the freezer, so you need to make sure that they are distributed evenly all around. Leave the bowls in the freezer overnight.

Unmold the two bowls by running warm water on them. You now have an ice bowl with embedded flowers. Place it in a plastic bag and keep it in the freezer until you need it.

Wash your fruit, let them dry, and cut them into cubes. Before you serve, place the ice bowl on a nice flat platter and fill it with fruit. Serve with whipped cream or sabayon and nuts.

Sabayon (French) or Zabaione (Italian) sauce 🌾

Sabayon is a fancy sauce. It is usually made with sweet wine, such as a Marsala, but can also be made with rum, Cointreau, or any other liquor. An exquisite version is made with Champagne and served with strawberries… It is memorable!

The origin of this sauce is Italy, and back in the day, they used to make it with whole eggs.

Most recipes now call for egg yolk only, but I like to use the whole egg because I think the texture is lighter. We cook the sauce over a Bain Marie (see page 6).

2 eggs (room temperature)
3 tablespoons sugar
2 tablespoons rum (or the liquor of your choice)
1/4 cup heavy cream

1. Place a pot with a little water over very low heat.

2. In a heat-proof bowl add the eggs and sugar and whisk with an electric handheld mixer until incorporated (do not leave the sugar with the eggs without whisking because sugar burns the egg yolk). Add the liquor and place the bowl over the simmering water (Bain Marie) while still whisking. We need to cook the sauce for about 5 minutes over water that is barely simmering. The eggs will cook and pasteurize, and the sauce will thicken up and be very warm if you touch it. The longer you cook, the thicker the sauce will become. In a separate bowl whisk the heavy cream until soft peaks form and field into the egg cream. Use the sauce within thirty minutes or refrigerate it. You can warm it up again just before serving. (If your sauce gets too thick just add a teaspoon of warm water and whisk).

Serve the sauce in a bowl next to the fruit salad.

You can find a version of Sabayon with only egg yolks (no whites) on page 99.

Maddie: One day Natasa brought out a crystal bowl with flowers in it and it was filled with fruit! But as I got closer I saw the bowl was ice! I took so many pictures of it!

Pavlova (8-12) 🌾

Pavlova is one of the most interesting and impressive desserts. It is a composition of sweet crunchy meringue, unsweetened smooth cream, and a variety of fresh, sour berries (usually) or other fruit. In short a wonderful contrast of textures and flavors.

Pavlova is not complicated, but it is technical since you need to adhere to rules to achieve a well-baked meringue, with a crispy exterior and soft interior, because a lot of things can go wrong. The rules for a successful meringue are:

1. It is best to use egg whites from eggs that have been separated from the yolks 2-3 days in advance and kept in the fridge in a jar, completely covered. "Old" eggs contain less moisture and they smell less, thus are ideal for the preparation of the meringue. (Egg whites may be stored in the fridge for up to 10 days). So plan ahead if you are preparing for a party.

2. Your utensils need to be completely dry with no trace of moisture. Notwithstanding what we have believed for many years, traces of fat (like egg yolk) would not affect the meringue.

3. Sugar should be added one tablespoon at a time AFTER the egg whites start to froth.

4. When you start whisking the egg whites, it is important to have a consistent medium speed and not turn your speed up and down, until the protein in the egg starts to stabilize. Therefore, a stand-up mixer is preferred to a handheld one.

5. A pinch of salt helps in stabilizing the protein.

6. Vinegar (or lemon juice) is essential.

7. Baking is extremely important in the success of a meringue. You need to experiment with your oven to find the best temperature for baking a meringue. Once you find it, note it and use it.

5 egg whites
100 grams or 1/2 cup sugar
125 grams or 1 cup powdered sugar
A pinch of salt
1 tablespoon cornstarch
1 tablespoon white vinegar or lemon juice
500 grams or 2 cups cream
1 tablespoon sugar
1 teaspoon vanilla extract
1 1/2 cups fruit of your choice (berries are a very good choice)

1. In a dry, clean bowl place the egg whites and start whisking at medium speed. When the mixture starts to froth, start adding the sugar a tablespoon at a time, first the regular and then the icing sugar and a pinch of salt. Be very careful to add the sugar gradually or your meringue will "weep" (moisture will come out like drops because the sugar will not be dissolved) when baked. When all the sugar is added, turn the speed up to medium-high.

2. Meanwhile, turn the oven to 250°F on the air setting. On parchment paper trace the desirable size of one big (10 or 11 inches), two medium (8 in.), or ten small (3 in.) individual circles with a pencil. Flip your paper over so that your meringue will not come in contact with

the pencil residues. Place the parchment paper on a cookie sheet.

3. You can stop whisking when you lift the whisk and the peak barely leans over or when you turn the bowl upside down and the meringue does not fall off. Fold in the cornstarch and vinegar with soft movements. Transfer the meringue to the parchment paper either with a piping bag or with a spatula following your drawing.

4. Transfer the uncooked meringue to the oven and bake for 90 minutes for small ones, 2 hours if you have two medium meringues, or 3 hours if you have a big one. Depending on your oven, the meringue may start to get a yellow color. If this happens, you will need to lower the temperature slightly and extend the cooking time.

5. Once a thick crust is created and the bottom of the meringue comes off the parchment paper easily, turn the oven off and leave the meringue in the oven to cool completely, preferably overnight. When completely cool, remove from the parchment paper and store in an airtight container or place carefully on a platter.

6. When you are ready to serve the pavlova, whisk the heavy cream with the vanilla and one tablespoon of sugar. When the whisk leaves its trail on the cream, stop whisking and transfer onto the meringue with a spatula or with your piping bag. Place the fruit on top and serve.

Consume within three or four hours of assembling. Pavlova will still be edible and tasty the following day, but the meringue will not be crunchy anymore.

Pavlova with fruit may or may not be lighter than just fruit...

Lemon Raspberry Swirl Cheesecake *(8)*

Crust
180 grams or 6 ounces digestive or Graham cookies or cookies of your choice
45grams or 3 tablespoons butter, melted
20 grams 2 tablespoons powdered sugar
1/8 teaspoon salt

Filling
250 grams or 8 ounces ricotta cheese
250 grams or 8 ounces cream cheese
14 ounces sweetened condensed milk
Zest of two lemons
170 grams or 3/4 cup lemon juice
1/2 cup raspberries (fresh or frozen)
2 gelatin sheets or 2 tsp gelatin powder if you are serving in a pan. You do not need to use gelatin if you serve in individual glasses.

1. Take the cheeses (ricotta and cream cheese) out of the fridge and leave them on the counter for 30-60 minutes before using or place your condensed milk in the fridge so they are at the same temperature.

2. Make the crust first. In the bowl of the food processor, place the cookies and pulse until they are well ground. Add the butter, powdered sugar, salt, and pulse until the mixture is smooth and homogenous. Transfer to a 9 x 11 inch baking dish and press with your hands to create a smooth surface. Bake for 15-20 minutes at 350°F. Let it cool completely.

3. Add the gelatin sheets to a bowl with water or the gelatin powder in 3 tablespoons of water.

4. Add the ricotta cheese, cream cheese, condensed milk, zest, and juice to the food processor and work until the resulting cream is completely smooth.

5. Warm up 4 tablespoons of water to approximately 140°F and add the gelatin. Stir well to fully dissolve gelatin. Add to the cheese mixture and mix very well.

6. Transfer all but half a cup of the cheese filling to the baking dish on top of the cookie crust.

7. If you are using frozen raspberries, let them thaw first on a kitchen paper towel to absorb the excess moisture. Place the raspberries in the food processor with the remaining half cup of the cheese mixture and pulse again until the mixture is smooth. Transfer to a piping bag and pipe a few lines on the lemon cheese cream. With a spoon blend and create beautiful swirls. Place in the refrigerator for at least 2 hours before you serve.

Tip: In case you want to serve your dessert in glasses, grind the cookies with sugar and salt, skip the butter, and divide them at the bottom of the glasses you are serving the dessert. Press the crumbs firmly and add the filling carefully. As mentioned above, you do not need to add gelatin if you are serving in individual bowls or glasses.

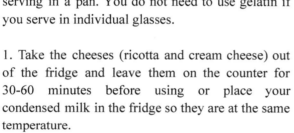

Cindee: *Similar to a lemony custard with a delicious buttery graham cracker crust. So, so good!*

Ekmek (12)

Cream Patisserie

960 grams or 4 cups milk (3.5% fat)

250 grams or 1 1/4 cup sugar

1/2 vanilla pod (do not use vanilla extract; you have to use a vanilla pod for this dessert)

4 eggs + 1 egg yolk

60 grams or 7 tablespoons flour PLUS 40 grams or 6 Tablespoons cornstarch

Base: Your choice of digestive cookies, white toast bread, ladyfingers, or plain cake. You can slice your base ingredient at any thickness you wish, I recommend around half an inch.

60 grams or 4 tablespoons melted butter

Syrup

200 grams or 1 cup water

200 grams or 1 cup sugar

Zest and juice of one orange

Topping

500 grams or 2 cups heavy cream

25 grams or 2 tablespoons sugar

Marmalade or fresh fruit, of your choice

Optional: pistachios or almonds

1. Make the cream first. Add the milk and the sugar to a pot and turn the heat to medium. Sugar forms a protective layer at the bottom of the pan that prevents the milk from burning, so don't stir to dissolve the sugar. Take half a vanilla stick, slice it in the middle, and scrape the seeds. Add the seeds and the half stick to the milk mixture. Save the other half stick in a jar with sugar to prevent it from drying. Let the milk steam, but do not let it boil.

2. In a bowl whisk the eggs, yolk, flour, and cornstarch (be precise in leveling measuring spoon) very well. When the milk starts to steam, start adding the milk, a ladle at a time, to the egg mixture while whisking with the other hand. When half of the milk is added to the eggs in the bowl, transfer the egg mixture to the pot. Turn the heat to low, and stir vigorously for 20 seconds. Cook, stirring constantly until the cream starts to thicken and bubbles form.

3. As soon as bubbles form, take the cream off the heat and transfer it to a clean bowl. Place a plastic wrap directly on the surface of the cream to keep moisture out. Your cream will stay fresh longer. Let the cream cool slightly and then place in the fridge for at least two hours.

4. Add all syrup ingredients to a pot and let them boil for five minutes. Take off the heat.

5. Butter generously a 9x11 inch pan and arrange the cookies on the bottom to create a base. Drizzle with melted butter. If you are using bread or cake, arrange in the pan and place them in the oven for ten minutes until a golden color is achieved. Take the pan out of the oven and immediately drizzle with the hot syrup. Let the base absorb the syrup and cool completely.

6. Take the cream out of the fridge and with a handheld mixer whisk it for 3 minutes to regain fluffiness. Spread on the base. For a fancier presentation, you can divide your base into 12 glasses. Add the syrup and let the base absorb it thoroughly and then add the cream.

7. Whisk the heavy cream with the sugar until stiff peaks form. Transfer to a piping bag and decorate on top of the cream. Add a little marmalade or fresh strawberries or bananas (favorite with our students), and finish with pistachios or almonds for a beautiful presentation.

Shannon: *You made some type of pudding that tasted like cinnamon and bananas,*
but it didn't have bananas in it. I liked it so much that I cleaned out the bowl.

Chocolate pudding (8-12)

Pudding
200 grams or 1 cup sugar
140 grams or 1 cup flour
960 grams or 4 cups milk
½ teaspoon salt
1 teaspoon pure vanilla extract
200 grams or 7 ounces dark chocolate (you may also use semi-sweet)
120 grams or 1 stick butter
4 gelatin sheets or 4 teaspoons gelatin powder (if you want to serve in a bundt form)

Caramelized nuts
200 grams or 1 cup sugar
3 tablespoons distilled or bottled water
1 cup pistachios or almonds or hazelnuts
A generous pinch of salt
Fruit of your choice: strawberries, cherries, or bananas work very well

1. Chop the chocolate and cut the butter into small cubes and place both in a bowl.
2. In another bowl add the sugar and flour and mix well. Add the cold milk, salt, and vanilla extract and mix thoroughly. Now transfer the mixture to a pot through a sieve (to catch any flour lumps). Turn the heat on at medium, stirring constantly to cook the mixture until it starts to thicken up to a pudding consistency. Bubbles will start to form on the surface and when they do, take the pudding off the heat and add the chopped chocolate and butter. Let it stand for five minutes for the chocolate and the butter to soften and start melting.
3. You have to decide how you are going to serve your pudding. You can serve it in small individual glasses or bowls or in a big bowl, in which case you don't need to add gelatin. The texture of the pudding will be delightfully silky. Your other option is to place the pudding in one big bundt cake form, let it set for a few hours, and serve it upside down. In this case, you need to add gelatin to your pudding so that it will unmold well. The pudding will be more impressive as seen in the picture. The texture will still be very pleasant but more jiggly. It is your choice.

If you are going to unmold the pudding and you are using gelatin sheets, add them to a small bowl with water to moisten them. If you are using gelatin powder, mix four teaspoons of gelatin powder with 6 tablespoons of milk. Let your gelatin moisten while you do step 4. Read the gelatin instructions on page 6 or the instructions on your gelatine box. We are proposing 4 gelatin sheets or teaspoons of powder for 4 cups of liquid, but this might differ for the gelatin brand you are using.

4. Back to the pudding: Stir until all the chocolate and the butter dissolve. If you are using individual bowls, divide the pudding into the bowls and decorate with a few caramelized nuts and fruit and serve. If you are using a bundt form, take the gelatin sheets out of the water. Squeeze them (discard the water) and add them to the mixture or add the gelatin powder mixed with milk. Stir well until all gelatin is dissolved. In the unfortunate event that your

mixture is not smooth, use a hand blender to break the lumps and then pass the mixture through a sieve. It is very important for the pudding to have a smooth texture. If you are using a bundt cake form, let the dessert set for at least three hours (or more) before you unmold and serve. Immerse the form in hot water for ten or fifteen seconds to facilitate the unmolding. Decorate with fruit and caramelized nuts and enjoy!

Caramelized Nuts: In a heavy saucepan add the sugar and three tablespoons of water and turn the heat to medium. Control the temperature of the pan by lifting it off the heat periodically for a few seconds (see page 8) if you see that the sugar starts to darken too rapidly. When all the sugar melts and turns into a golden caramel (take care that it does not turn brown) add the nuts and salt and stir until all the nuts are coated with a transparent golden caramel. Ideally, before you add the nuts to the caramel you need to warm them in another saucepan, or the shock of the cold nuts will harden the caramel too fast. When all the nuts are coated with the caramel transfer them onto aluminum foil or parchment paper and wait for them to cool completely. Be very careful how you handle the caramel because it is extremely hot and can cause severe burns.

Cindee: Three bites of heaven... So rich and chocolaty...

Orange Cupcakes with Jello Domes (12)

Dough

200 grams or 14 tablespoons unsalted butter, room temperature

200 grams or 1 cup sugar

4 eggs

1/2 teaspoon orange zest

120 grams or 1/2 cup orange juice

120 grams or 1/2 cup heavy cream

A pinch of salt

1 teaspoon baking powder

200 grams or 1 1/2 cups flour

Jello Domes

200 grams or 1 cup sugar

400 grams or 2 cups water

Zest of one orange

4 cups brewed spice tea OR white wine

12 gelatin sheets or 12 teaspoons of gelatin powder (or read instructions on the package)

2 cups of fruit (Orange fillets and an assortment of red fruit, berries, or pomegranate)

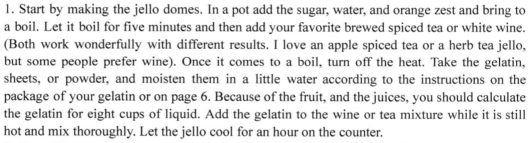

1. Start by making the jello domes. In a pot add the sugar, water, and orange zest and bring to a boil. Let it boil for five minutes and then add your favorite brewed spiced tea or white wine. (Both work wonderfully with different results. I love an apple spiced tea or a herb tea jello, but some people prefer wine). Once it comes to a boil, turn off the heat. Take the gelatin, sheets, or powder, and moisten them in a little water according to the instructions on the package of your gelatin or on page 6. Because of the fruit, and the juices, you should calculate the gelatin for eight cups of liquid. Add the gelatin to the wine or tea mixture while it is still hot and mix thoroughly. Let the jello cool for an hour on the counter.

2. Use silicone, round forms or look for 12 glasses with a nice round interior form and use them. The diameter of your molds (or glasses) should not be more than 2.5 inches. Divide the jello into the 12 molds and place them in the fridge for 20 minutes to set slightly. Take out of the fridge and arrange the orange fillet and red fruit into the molds. Take them back to the fridge and let them set for at least four hours. Unmold by inserting them briefly in hot water or letting hot water run over them. Keep in the fridge covered, until ready to use.

3. Preheat the oven to 350°F. In the mixer bowl, add the butter and sugar and whisk until light and fluffy, approximately 5-7 minutes. Add the eggs one at a time. Mix for another five minutes, then lower the speed and add the orange zest, juice, and cream. Work the mixture until it is smooth, and turn the mixer off. Fold in the flour, salt, and baking powder. Partition the batter to a muffin tray (buttered or lined with paper cupcake cups) and bake for 30 minutes. When completely cool, place one jello dome onto every cupcake and serve.

Orange fillet. Remove the peel and the white exterior membrane with the help of a sharp, paring knife. Hold the peeled orange and cut the orange fillet out of the membrane, by inserting the knife in the orange, next to a membrane. Insert again on the other side of the same slice, next to the opposite membrane, creating a V shape, as shown in the picture above.

Alex: The coolest - in every sense of the word - cupcake I have ever had...

Strawberry Jello (8-12) 🌾 🥛

When my son was little this was his favorite dessert for his birthday, which is the beginning of May, strawberry season. As easy and lovely as it can be, we forget just how delicious it is.

2 packages of strawberry jello
500 grams or 1 pound strawberries
Topping:
 240 grams or 1 cup heavy cream (Skip topping ingredients if lactose intolerant)
120 grams or 1/2 cup cream cheese or mascarpone
2 tablespoons powdered sugar

1. Read the instructions on your jello packaging and make the jello accordingly, reducing the water by 1/4 of what is instructed. For example, if instructions call for 4 cups of water, use three. The fruit might produce some moisture, so we add less water. This keeps us from compromising the density of our jello and ensuring that it unmolds well.
2. Wash the strawberries and cut them in halves or in fourths.
3. Fill up a dish (a bundt cake form or a big bowl will do) with 1/3 of the jello. Allow it to set for 15 minutes in the fridge. Place the strawberries in the dish. You may want to keep the stem on a few strawberries for decoration. Place the ones with the stem first at the bottom. Fill with the rest of the jello and refrigerate for at least three hours.
4. Unmold by placing the dish in warm water for 10 seconds. Turn the dish upside down over a platter. Whisk the heavy cream with cream cheese, and powdered sugar until the whisk leaves a trail and the mixture has thickened up. Transfer to a piping bag and decorate your dessert. You may use as much or as little of this delicious cream as you wish.

Mosaic (8)

This is a favorite for Greek children. Turns out it is a big hit with American students, too.

250 grams or 2 sticks of butter
240 grams or 8 ounces dark chocolate
80 grams or 1/2 cup cocoa powder
40 grams or 1/4 cup powdered sugar
3 tablespoons rum or 3 tablespoons fresh orange juice
1 teaspoon vanilla extract
A generous pinch of sea salt
300 grams or 10 ounces digestive cookies or graham cookies or cookies of your choice

1. Place a pot over *very* low heat and add the butter and chocolate. Be attentive while the butter and chocolate melt and stir often. (Alternatively, you may use Bain Marie, see page 6). After they melt add the cocoa powder, powdered sugar, rum or orange juice, vanilla extract, and salt. Mix well and let the chocolate mixture cool for 15-20 minutes.

2. In a bowl cut the digestive cookies (or other cookies of your choice) into approximately one-inch square chunks. Use a knife so that they do not crumble too much.

3. Add the cookies to the chocolate mixture and mix. Take a big piece of parchment paper or plastic wrap and lay it in a rectangular cake form. Transfer the mixture to the cake form. Fold the paper over the chocolate mixture enclosing it completely. Freeze it for 30 minutes, take it out of the freezer and holding the two ends of the paper roll the chocolate "sausage" a couple of times to create a nice chocolate sausage before you take it back to the freezer. You may keep the Mosaic in the freezer for a couple of months or in the fridge for several days.

I happen to have a cylindrical flower form for bread, so I use it for this dessert.

Bryce: *The best Mosaic in Greece!*

Dorothea's cookies (24)

My aunt Dorothea, whom I loved dearly, served tea every night. On the many occasions I was at her home for the nighttime tea ritual, she would offer these incredible cookies. The transparency of the marmalade in the middle of the cookie mesmerized my childish eyes. I don't know if these cookies sparked my love for transparent objects (aka crystal) or if my love for transparent objects fueled my obsession with these cookies. In any case, I loved them, and I love sharing the recipe. You may use any marmalade or jam you like, but the orange marmalade (which is my favorite) offers bitterness, a contrast with the almondy cookies, and freshness to the mouth that is so appealing to me.

350 grams or 3 sticks minus 1 tablespoon butter (left on the counter for 30 minutes)
150 grams or 1 cup plus 1 tablespoon powdered sugar
1 teaspoon pure vanilla extract
1 egg
A pinch of salt
150 grams or 1 1/2 cup almond powder (finely grated almonds)
350 grams or 2 2/3 cups flour

1 cup of marmalade of your choice: orange, strawberry, and apricot are good options

1. A very important parameter for the success of the cookies is the temperature of the butter. Take it out of the fridge 30 minutes before using it. We want it to be around 50°F. In a mixer bowl add the butter and sugar and whisk at medium speed until the mixture takes a light yellow color and turns fluffy around 10 minutes. Add the vanilla extract, egg, and salt and whisk some more.
2. Sift (very important to sift) the flour with the almond powder. In the mixer turn the speed down to the slowest and add the sifted flours until just incorporated.
3. Place the dough between two parchment papers or sil pats and roll it to a thickness of 1/4 inch. Place in the fridge for 30 minutes for the dough to harden.
4. Cut out cookies with a round cookie cutter or a flower-shaped one that is about two or three inches in diameter. For half of the cookies, cut out a hole in the middle with the help of a piping nozzle. You will need to refrigerate the dough again if it starts to warm up and soften.
5. Butter a cookie sheet or line it with parchment paper and arrange the unbaked cookies on it. Bake the cookies at 300°F for 20 minutes until the bottom of the cookie is not stuck to the parchment paper anymore but the color is still light. The edges should not have turned golden.
6. Let the cookies cool completely and spread a teaspoon of marmalade on half of the cookies (the whole ones). Place the cookies with the hole over the cookies with marmalade to make a cookie sandwich. Sprinkle with some powdered sugar.
7. Dip them in tea.

Malebi (6) 🌾

The following desserts are very popular in Middle Eastern cultures, as they are tasty, healthy, and very easy to make. Malebi is a creamy dessert made with milk or Almond milk, cornstarch, and one ingredient of your choice for flavoring. The most common flavoring is mastic (mastiha). Mastic* is a resin with amazing healing and beautifying properties and it is uniquely Greek product. Note that for every 8 cups of liquid, you need one cup of cornstarch.

4 cups of milk. You may use any kind of milk you prefer. Almond milk works well, too.

1/2 cup cornstarch

Options: Choose ONE of the options for four cups of liquid:

1) 4 tablespoons strawberry jam

2) 4 tablespoons orange marmalade

3) 1 teaspoon pure vanilla extract + 4 tablespoons sugar

4) 4 tablespoons sugar + 1 teaspoon flower water (I prefer jasmine over rose water)

5) 1 teaspoon cinnamon + 4 tablespoons sugar

6) 80 grams or 2 1/2 ounces chopped chocolate + 2-4 tablespoons sugar

7) 6-8 pearls of mastic, crushed with 4 tablespoons sugar

1. Prepare, meaning choose four big glasses or six medium ones.

2. In a pot add cold milk and cornstarch and mix well until the cornstarch is dissolved.

3. Turn the heat on to medium and start stirring. If you are using one of the last four options, add the ingredients now. Keep stirring until your cream thickens up. If you are using one of the first four ingredients, add them after your cream thickens up. After adding the ingredient of your choice, mix well and divide the dessert into glasses. Let the Malebi cool. Refrigerate for a couple of hours and consume cold. They keep well for a few days.

Variation: Orange Juice Malebi (6)

In the same spirit, you can substitute milk with fresh orange juice or lemon juice. A very refreshing and unique treat for summer days.

2 cups freshly squeezed orange juice
2 cups water
1/2 cup cornstarch
3/4 cup of sugar
Ground pistachio or chocolate for decoration

Mix the orange juice, water, cornstarch, and sugar in a pot and stir well before you turn on the heat. Place over medium heat and start stirring constantly. It will take 4-5 minutes for your cream to thicken up. As soon as it bubbles, take it off the heat. Serve in individual glasses and decorate with chocolate or ground pistachio.

If you want to make it with lemon juice use: 1 cup lemon juice, 3 cups water, 1/2 cup cornstarch and 1 cup sugar.

***Mastic gum** can only be produced on the island of Chios, in Greece. Mastic (Μαστίχα) has been used for its therapeutic and beautifying properties since antiquity. It was first used during the Ottoman Empire in pastries for its delicate evergreen aroma. If you live in the US you can order it through apollogum.com.*

Plum Cake (8-12)

45 grams or 3 tablespoons butter
100 grams or 1/2 cup light brown sugar
6 plums (1 pound of fruit). Plums vary greatly in sweetness and juiciness, so you have to use your judgment: if your plums are very sour, add two additional tablespoons of sugar.

120 grams or 1 stick butter (room temperature)
200 grams or 1 cup sugar
1 teaspoon pure vanilla extract
Zest of half an orange
A pinch of salt
3 egg yolks
200 grams or 1 1/2 cups flour
1 tablespoon baking powder
100 grams or 1/2 cup yogurt (2% or 5% fat)
3 egg whites

1. Preheat the oven to 420°F. Butter a springform cake pan and line it with parchment paper or place parchment paper at the bottom of a round pan to facilitate the unmolding of the cake. Parchment paper helps create a caramelized surface on the cake.
2. Melt 3 tablespoons of butter and transfer to the bottom of the pan. Sprinkle the brown sugar evenly over the butter. Wash the plums and cut each one into six or eight wedges, depending on the size, removing the pit. Arrange one layer of plums neatly at the bottom of the pan, over the sugar, and add a second layer, too.
3. Place the stick of butter in the mixer bowl along with the sugar and beat at medium speed until the mixture becomes lighter in color, around 5-7 minutes. Make sure you scrape the sides of the bowl periodically. Add the vanilla extract, orange zest, salt, and three yolks and beat until fully incorporated.
4. Turn the mixer to the lowest speed. Mix the flour with the baking powder in a small bowl. Add 1/3 of the flour mixture and half of the yogurt to the batter and mix. Add the other 1/3 of the flour and the rest of the yogurt and mix again. Finish by adding the rest of the four, and mixing until just incorporated.
5. In a clean and dry bowl, add the three egg whites and beat until stiff peaks are formed.
6. Fold the egg whites into the cake batter carefully, and when all are incorporated, transfer the batter to the pan and level the top. Tap the pan lightly until you see air bubbles coming to the surface. We want the trapped air to escape so that our cake is as smooth as possible.
7. Place the cake in the oven and bake for 10 minutes. Turn the temperature down to 380°F and bake for another 40-45 minutes or until a knife comes out clean when inserted in the middle of the cake. Let it cool for at least 15 minutes before you unmold it. Run a knife around the sidewall to loosen the sides. Place a platter on the cake form and, holding both firmly, platter and form, flip upside down. Remove the parchment paper and serve with heavy cream or ice cream.

Andrew: Angels would shed tears over this cake!

Strawberries with Cream and Soil (6) 🌾

You can substitute this cream with plain whipped cream for this fun dessert.

<u>Cream</u> (For six small glasses)
1 egg
40 grams or 3 tablespoons sugar
15 grams or 3 teaspoons cornstarch
180 grams or 3/4 cup milk
1/2 teaspoon pure vanilla extract
25 grams or 1 1/2 tablespoons butter
<u>Strawberry Compote</u>
600 grams or 21 ounces strawberries
60 grams or 5 tablespoons sugar
<u>Chocolate "Soil"</u>
100 grams or 1/2 cup sugar
3 tablespoons water
70 grams or 2.5 ounces chocolate chopped into small pieces
1/4 teaspoon salt

1. Whisk the egg with the sugar and cornstarch very well.

2. In a pot warm up the milk until it starts to steam. Add half of the hot milk to the egg mixture. Stir well and then transfer the egg mixture to the pot with the rest of the milk. Stir vigorously for 20 seconds and then, over very low heat, continue stirring until the cream bubbles. Remove immediately and transfer the cream to a clean bowl. Add the vanilla extract and cold butter and mix well, until the cream is smooth. Cover with plastic wrap directly on the surface of the cream and place in the fridge until thoroughly cold.

3. Wash the strawberries, remove the stem, and cut them into half-inch squares. Place in a metal bowl. Add the sugar (sugar should be 1/10 of the strawberry weight) and stir. Cover the bowl with plastic wrap to seal it completely. Place the sealed bowl over a pot with water over very low heat (Bain-Marie, see page 6) and let the strawberries cook with the steam of the simmering pot for 20 minutes. Take the bowl off the heat, and let the strawberries cool completely before removing the plastic wrap. You can keep them in the fridge for 3-4 days.

4. In a heavy saucepan, add the sugar and water over medium heat. Swirl the pan around but do not stir the sugar. Let the temperature of the caramel reach 260°F (the caramel will start to turn from golden to brown). Take the saucepan off the stove and immediately add the chocolate and the salt. It is very important that the chocolate is chopped into very small pieces, less than half an inch squares. Mix very well and continue mixing and breaking the lumps until the mixture starts to cool down and resemble soil. Essentially we are burning the chocolate with the caramel. If your caramel had not reached the right temperature when you added the chocolate, it would remain liquid and would not turn into soil. In this case, spread on parchment paper, let it cool completely, and place it in a food processor to create "sand".

5. Divide the strawberries across 6 small glasses. Add the cream, using a piping bag in a spiral motion, starting from the edge of the glass and going in towards the middle (if you start in the middle the cream will sink in the strawberry mixture). Top with the chocolate soil. Cover with plastic wrap and refrigerate. Before you serve, decorate with edible flowers and green leaves.

Aiden: *My cousin used to eat dirt, but I think she would find this soil more delicious and nutritious…*
On the real, this soil is the perfect crumbly chocolate addition to everything.

Tart with Almond cream (8)

Pie Crust for 9 or 10-inch dish
200 grams or 1 1/2 cups flour
A pinch of salt
15 grams or 1 tablespoon of sugar
120 grams or 1 stick cold butter cut into cubes
2 tablespoons cold water
Almond Cream
240 grams or 2 sticks butter (room temperature)
250 grams or 2 cups powdered sugar
250 grams or 2 1/2 cups almond powder
250 grams or 5 eggs
1 teaspoon pure vanilla extract
1/2 teaspoon almond extract (optional) OR 25 grams or 2 tablespoons rum
A pinch of salt
50 grams or 6 tablespoons flour
1.5 cups fresh fruit of your choice (or nuts, read end of page)
Powdered sugar for dusting

1. Place the flour, salt, and sugar in a food processor and mix. Add the cold butter, cut in cubes, and pulse a few times until a sand-like mixture is created. Add one tablespoon of cold water and pulse. Then a second tablespoon and pulse again. Check to see if the dough holds together. It might need a few more drops of water. As soon as it holds together, take the dough out of the food processor and press it together to form a ball. Roll the dough in between two parchment papers, dusting with a little flour as needed. Place it in the fridge on a cookie sheet, wrapped in parchment paper or plastic wrap, for at least 30 minutes.
2. Turn the oven to 380°F.
3. Transfer the dough to a pie dish (9 or 10-inch diameter), prick with a fork several times, and bake for 15 minutes.
4. While the dough is baking, prepare the cream. Place the butter and the sugar in the mixer bowl and whisk on medium speed until the color of the mixture becomes light yellow.
5. Turn the mixer to low and gradually add the almond powder, eggs (one by one), vanilla, and salt. If you want to accentuate the almond flavor even more add a little almond extract or if you prefer add rum. Turn the mixer off and fold the flour into the mixture.
6. By now your pie crust should have started to take on a nice golden color. Take it out of the oven and transfer the almond cream onto the pie shell. Bake for 35-40 more minutes until your cream turns a nice golden color. Let it cool completely, and then decorate it with fruit. Dust with powdered sugar. You can serve it plain or with ice cream or Greek yogurt.
Another version of this tart is baked with fruits. Choose fruits that do not produce a lot of moisture, like plums, pears, apricots, and figs, or, alternatively use nuts. Arrange them on the almond cream before baking it. Proceed with baking the pie with the almond cream and the fruit or nuts and serving it warm.

Ann: This CREAM!! I did not expect so much taste in a single bite...

Tip: Have you noticed that the dough starts to stick to your new tart pans after two or three uses? Unfortunately, this happens because our cleaning agents, especially the dishwasher soap, destroy the protective film of the pan that prevents the dough from sticking to it. Wash your tart pan in warm water and a little soap with a very soft cloth by hand, and it will be as good as new for many years to come.

Strawberry and Lemon Tart (8-10) 🖾

Base
150 grams or 1 1/2 cups almond powder or 1 1/4 cups of blanched almonds
50 grams or 1/4 cup sugar
110 grams or 1/2 cup extra virgin olive oil or 1 stick butter (both work well)
A pinch of salt
1 teaspoon pure vanilla extract
200 grams or 1 1/2 cup flour
Lemon Curd
200 grams or 1 cup sugar
5 egg yolks
200 grams or 1 cup lemon juice
3 gelatin sheets or 3 teaspoons of gelatin powder
60 grams or 1/2 stick butter (optional)
Zest of 2 lemons
2 tablespoons Grand Marnier Liqueur
Swiss Meringue
5 egg whites
200 grams or 1 cup sugar
1000 grams or 2 pounds strawberries

1. In a food processor bowl, add blanched almonds and sugar and work until they resemble a fine sand texture. Alternatively, you can use almond powder, which is almonds already grated to a fine texture, exactly what we need for this tart. Preheat the oven to 380°F.

2. Add the olive oil or butter (cold), salt, and vanilla extract. Pulse until all ingredients are combined. Add the flour and pulse once or twice. Check if the dough holds together and add one or two tablespoons of water if it does not. If you are using olive oil it probably will not need any water. This dough is crumbly and cannot be rolled easily because of the almond powder, so spread it by hand, as evenly as possible, in a 9-inch buttered (or oiled) pie shell. If you are using olive oil, you do not need to chill the crust. If you are using butter, chill the crust for 30 minutes. You may also make small, individual tartelettes.

3. Prick the base with a fork several times. Bake for 40-45 minutes, or until the crust is golden brown. Let the crust cool completely.

4. Make the Lemon Curd. In a metal bowl over Bain Marie (page 6) add the sugar, 5 yolks, and lemon juice and whisk over simmering water for 4-5 minutes. As soon as the mixture thickens up slightly (it will not thicken up to a cream consistency) and a thermometer shows 175°F, if you have one, take the bowl off the heat and place it over a bath of ice water to help in lowering the temperature fast. Place the gelatin sheets in a bowl with cold water to moisten the gelatin or add the gelatin powder to half a cup of water. Three to five minutes later add the gelatin to the cream according to the instructions on page 6. Mix very well to dissolve completely. Cut the butter into small cubes and add it along with the lemon zest and, if you are using it, the Grand Marnier, and stir well. The butter adds flavor and richness, but it is not essential. If you are serving people with dairy allergies, skip it. Place a plastic wrap on the surface and let the curd cool down and set.

5. Swiss Meringue. Place the 5 egg whites and 1 cup sugar in a clean bowl and take the bowl over a pot with simmering water—a Bain Marie. Whisk with a handheld mixer until the mixture reaches 150°F. You will see that it thickens up noticeably, resembling a marshmallow spread. Place the meringue in the bowl of the standing mixer and whisk at low speed, while it cools down, for another 10 minutes and then transfer it to a piping bag.

6. Whisk the lemon curd with a handheld mixer for 2 minutes to regain fluffiness. Transfer it to the pie shell and level the top. Arrange the strawberries either standing or lying on the curd, and finish by piping the meringue on the strawberries. With a torch, burn the meringue or broil it in the oven for 3-5 minutes, to create an interesting and tasty topping.

Cindee: A cross between flan, baklava, and a toasted marshmallow! Oh, my!!

Blueberry Cheesecake (12) 🌾

1 package digestive cookies (you will use 8 ounces of digestive cookies or the cookies of your choice. You may use gluten-free cookies for a gluten-free dessert)
2 tablespoons unsalted butter
1/8 teaspoon salt

Filling
250 grams or 9 ounces cream cheese
250 grams or 9 ounces ricotta cheese (mascarpone works, too)
3 tablespoons lemon juice
Zest of one lemon
2 eggs
150 grams or 3/4 cup sugar
1 teaspoon pure vanilla extract
30 grams or 3 tablespoons powdered sugar
150 grams or 5 ounces blueberries

1. Wash the blueberries. Place them on kitchen paper and let them dry.
2. Turn the oven on at 380°F.
3. Melt the butter and set it aside to cool. In a food processor, add the cookies and blend until the mixture resembles coarse sand. Add the butter and salt and pulse until it is thoroughly mixed. Take 3/4 of a cup of the crumbs and save it for later. Place the rest of the crushed cookies n a 9-inch pie dish that you have already buttered and press the crumbs into a crust as evenly and as neatly as you can.
4. In the food processor, add the cheeses and pulse. Add the lemon juice and zest, eggs, sugar, and vanilla and mix until the mixture is completely smooth.
5. Transfer the cheese mixture to the crust in the pie shell and even the top. Sprinkle one tablespoon of powdered sugar on the blueberries and mix so that the sugar coats the blueberries. Spread the blueberries on the cheese mixture as evenly as possible. Finish by sprinkling the crumbs that we saved earlier, on the cheesecake. Transfer to the oven and bake for 45-50 minutes until the cheesecake is golden brown and the mixture has set. Let it cool down completely and dust with a couple tablespoons of powdered sugar.

Tip: Strawberries, Raspberries, Blueberries—Without cutting the stems off, place the fruit in a bath of cold water (just covering them) and add a couple of tablespoons of red wine vinegar. Leave it for 4-5 minutes. The vinegar will kill any mold, and the fruit will stay fresh for many days. Rinse the fruit and keep it in the fridge on a paper towel in a bowl. Remove the stems (for strawberries) just before you are ready to consume them.

*Four-year-old **Edith,** asking every day, for the whole three months she was in Greece with her parents:*
Is TODAY blueberry cheesecake day, yet???

Lemon chiboust and Blackberries (10)

This base made from baked Swiss Meringue is wonderful. Light and crunchy is a perfect option for a tart base if you are going to add cream and fruit.

Swiss Meringue

5 egg whites

300 grams or 1 1/2 cups sugar

A pinch of salt

25 grams or 3 tablespoons flour

5 grams or 1 teaspoon red wine vinegar

Lemon Chiboust cream

120 grams or 1/2 cup and 2 tablespoons lemon juice

120 grams or 1/2 cup heavy cream

5 egg yolks

50 grams or 1/4 cup sugar

50 grams or 7 tablespoons cornstarch

Zest of two lemons

240 grams or 1 cup heavy cream

1 cup Blackberries for filling and decoration

1. Make the cream first. In a pot add the lemon juice and cream and warm it over very low heat. Do not worry if it curdles at this point. In another bowl add the yolks with the sugar, cornstarch, and zest and mix very well. When the lemon-cream mixture starts to steam, take one ladle scoop and add it to the egg yolks. Mix well. Take another ladle scoop and do the same. Then transfer the egg yolk mixture to the lemon-cream pot, mixing very well. Continue whisking until the mixture thickens up substantially. Take it off the heat immediately. In case there are lumps (which means that our egg yolks cooked too fast) blend with a handheld blender to regain a silky and wonderful texture. Place plastic wrap directly on the surface of the cream and transfer it to the fridge for at least two hours or, better, overnight.

2. Turn the oven to 300°F. Make the Swiss meringue. Add a little water to a pot and bring to a very soft boil. In a metal bowl, place egg whites, sugar, and salt and start whisking with a handheld mixer. Bring it over the boiling water (Bain Marie) and continue whisking until the mixture reaches 150°F. It will be thick and shiny, like a marshmallow spread. Transfer the meringue to a standing mixer and let it whisk for 10 minutes at a low speed. In the meantime, prepare a piece of parchment paper by cutting it into 12x14 inches and greasing it lightly.

3. After the meringue has been whisked for 10 minutes (it will be considerably cooler), sift in the flour, add the vinegar, and fold. Transfer to a piping bag (for a neater result) or use a spatula to shape the meringue into a half-inch thick rectangle on the parchment paper. Place it in the oven and bake for 16-18 minutes. If it starts to turn yellow, lower the temperature slightly. After 18-20 minutes turn the oven off. Check if the meringue peels off the parchment paper and if it does not let it cool in the oven for 20 minutes.

4. Take it out and flip it onto another piece of parchment paper. Very carefully peel off the paper it was baked on, but leave it on the meringue to prevent it from drying out. Cover with a kitchen towel and let it cool.

5. Whisk 1 cup of heavy cream. While still whisking, add the cold lemon cream a little at a time, and whisk until the texture is light and fluffy, 4-5 minutes. Spread the cold cream onto the baked meringue. Add blackberries in a row along the long side where you will start the rolling and with the help of the parchment paper roll it lightly to create a log. For a fancier presentation, you may blend 4 or 5 blackberries with half of the lemon chiboust to make some beautiful pink cream. Transfer the two creams into two piping bags and decorate with both creams (alternating yellow and pink), inside the yole and on top. Add blackberries and a few spearmint leaves.

Another option is to create small round disks with the Swiss meringue, bake them, pipe lemon chiboust and decorate them with cream and fruit. It is a beautiful presentation for a party, as individual pastries become finger food.

Cindee: A Greek Pavlova! Could be served in a five-star restaurant! Yummy

Berries and Vanilla Namelaka (8)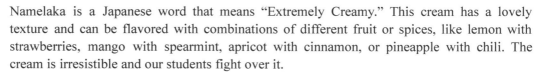

Namelaka is a Japanese word that means "Extremely Creamy." This cream has a lovely texture and can be flavored with combinations of different fruit or spices, like lemon with strawberries, mango with spearmint, apricot with cinnamon, or pineapple with chili. The cream is irresistible and our students fight over it.

500 grams or 21 ounces white chocolate
300 grams or 1 1/3 cups whole milk
5 gelatin sheets or 5 teaspoons gelatin powder
600 grams or 2 1/2 cups cream
1/4 teaspoon salt
1/2 cup blueberries (fresh or frozen) pureed
1/2 cup raspberries (fresh or frozen) pureed

1. In a pot warm up the milk. In a small bowl add cold water and the gelatin sheets or dissolve the gelatin powder in half cup of water.
2. Chop up the chocolate very finely. Place it, preferably, in a tall and narrow container and add the warm milk. Squeeze the water off the gelatin sheets and add them or add the moistened gelatin powder. With a handheld blender (that is why we prefer a tall container), whisk the mixture for 5 minutes. We want the blender to always touch the bottom of the container and not go up and down because we do not want air incorporated into our mixture.
3. Add the cream and salt and continue whisking for another 3 minutes. This whisking will create a wonderfully smooth texture in our cream. This texture is what defines Namelaka.
4. Take out 1/3 of the mixture and divide it across 8 glasses. Place the glasses in the fridge for 30 minutes until the cream is set. Keep the rest of the cream on the counter.
5. Take out of the container another 1/3 of the mixture, add the pureed blueberries, and mix thoroughly. Divide into the serving glasses, on top of the plain mixture. Place in the fridge until it is set, too.
6. Finally whisk the pureed raspberries in the last batch and divide that mixture on top of the other two layers. Decorate with fresh fruit and spearmint leaves or with cat tongues.

Cat Tongues (Austrian cookie often consumed with ganache or ice cream)
120 grams or 1 stick butter
150 grams or 1 1/4 cups powdered sugar
1/2 teaspoon vanilla extract
4 egg whites
120 grams or 1 cup flour

1. In a mixer whisk the butter, powdered sugar, and vanilla until very light in color. Line two cookie sheets with parchment paper and butter them lightly. Turn the oven to 390°F.
2. In another bowl, whisk the egg whites until stiff peaks are formed. Fold the egg whites into the butter mixture and sift in the flour. Fold and mix thoroughly. Transfer to a piping bag and pipe two-inch elongated cookies, using a 1/4-inch nozzle, on the cookie sheets. Bake them for 9-10 minutes or until the edges start to darken. Take them out of the oven and immediately place them on a curved object (like a bottle lying horizontally) to cool in the desired shape.

The Calm

The Storm

Strawberry Trifle (12-16)

Trifles are great desserts for a party because the individual preparations can be made ahead of time and assembled at the last minute. Choux puff is a versatile preparation and can be made two or three days in advance. Pastry cream can also be made two days in advance.

Choux Puffs OR you may use your favorite cookie
100 grams or 1/2 cup milk minus 2 tablespoons
100 grams or 1/2 cup water
1/2 teaspoon sugar
1/2 teaspoon salt
100 grams or 7 tablespoons butter
120 grams or 1 cup flour
3 or 4 eggs
Pastry Cream
1200 grams or 5 cups milk
240 grams or 1 cup cream
½ vanilla bean
200 grams or 1 cup sugar
80 grams or 1 cup cornstarch
6 egg yolks
3 whole eggs
Ganache
360 grams or 1 1/2 cups cream
400 grams or 14 ounces dark chocolate, chopped
1/8 teaspoon salt
2 cups Strawberries for decorations

1. **Choux Puffs**: In a medium pot add the water, milk, sugar, salt, and butter (cut in very small pieces because we want the butter to have melted before the liquid starts to boil) and stir to dissolve the salt and sugar. Bring to a boil. Let it boil for 2 minutes and take off the heat. Add the flour all at once, and stir vigorously until it is all absorbed and there are no clumps. Return the pot to the fire and continue stirring until the dough turns into a ball and a film of dough is formed at the bottom of the pan. Remove from the heat.
2. Place the dough in a mixer bowl and, with the kneading hook, start stirring at low speed.
3. Turn the oven to 375°F.
4. A few minutes later, when the dough has cooled down a little, add the eggs, one at a time while still mixing. Wait for one egg to be fully incorporated before you add the next one. When all the eggs are incorporated, the dough should look shiny and elastic. Stir for 2 more minutes. Before you add the last egg check the dough. If it looks shiny it might not need the fourth egg, especially if your eggs are bigger than medium.
5. Transfer the dough to a piping bag with a nozzle of around 1/4 of an inch in diameter. Place parchment paper on a cookie sheet, and butter it lightly. Start piping, creating small, walnut-size balls. Bake for 30 minutes until golden brown and then, briefly, open the oven

door, and with your sharpest knife prick the top of every pastry once to allow the trapped moisture to escape so that they do not collapse later (do not open the oven door before the 30 minutes). Let the choux bake for 5-10 more minutes. Take them out of the oven and let them cool completely. You may store them for a few days in an airtight container.

6. **Pastry cream**: In a pot, warm the milk, cream, and half the vanilla bean and seeds (scrape the seeds off first). I would urge you to use a vanilla bean and not the extract for this dessert.

7. In a bowl, whisk the sugar, cornstarch, eggs, and yolks. As soon as the milk starts to steam, take a ladle of the milk and add it to the egg mixture. Mix and add a second ladleful and then a third, mixing very well after each addition. Transfer the egg yolk mixture to the pot and vigorously mix for 20 seconds. Turn the heat to low and continue stirring. As soon as the first bubble forms, take it off the heat, and transfer it to a clean bowl. Place the bowl over an ice bath to lower the temperature. Cover with plastic wrap directly on top of the cream, so that your cream is protected from moisture and it will keep longer. Let the cream cool completely, preferably overnight, in the refrigerator.

8. On the day you will serve the dessert, make the **Ganache**. Warm up the cream with the salt, and when it steams, pour over a clean bowl in which you have placed the chopped chocolate.

Wait for 3 minutes for the chocolate to soften and then stir until all the chocolate melts and turns into a chocolate sauce, Ganache. Let it cool down to thicken for at least one hour.

9. Whisk the Pastry cream for 2-3 minutes to regain fluffiness (do not skip this step). Place a layer of pastry cream at the bottom of a big bowl. Remove the stems from the strawberries and place a layer of strawberries on the cream, standing up. Add the small choux puffs on top of the strawberries, or use cookies (shortbread cookies work well). Transfer the rest of the cream onto the choux puffs or cookies and finish your dessert with a thick layer of ganache. Decorate the top with whipped cream and strawberries or other berries and you have an impressive (and tasty) party dessert.

Bryce: It's like a strawberry shortcake, but with chocolate. I think it's my favorite dessert!

Feta cheese mousse (8-12) 🌾

Feta cheese is a favorite Greek product, and this is a fascinating way to serve it. Just so tasty and versatile.

300 grams or 10 ounces feta cheese
60 grams or 1/4 cup cream cheese or ricotta cheese
30 grams or 1/4 cup powdered sugar OR zest of a lemon and 1/2 teaspoon Tabasco sauce
240 grams or 1 cup heavy cream
1 package of really good, savory crackers

Options for serving.
1) 1 cup cherry tomatoes and basil leaves, olive oil and balsamic vinegar, a pinch of salt, 1 tablespoon poppy seeds
2) 6 figs, 12 slices bacon, 2 tablespoons olive oil, and 2 tablespoons balsamic vinegar
3) 1 big slice of watermelon, a pinch of salt, poppy seeds
4) 6 pears, 12 slices of prosciutto and poppy seeds

1. In a food processor, place the feta and 1/4 cup cream cheese or ricotta cheese. Blend until the mixture is completely smooth. Add the powdered sugar and blend some more if you are serving the three last options. If you are serving cherry tomatoes, add the zest of a lemon and then Tabasco sauce to taste.
2. Whip 1 cup heavy cream to medium consistency and fold into the feta mixture. Divide into the smallest ice cube holders you have and place them in the freezer. Let them stay in the freezer for at least one hour. Unmold and serve on a cracker with the topping of your choice. If you are serving the mousse on another day, keep it in the freezer. When ready to serve, unmold the feta mousse and place it in the fridge for 15 minutes. Decorate on a platter with the topping of your choice just before you serve. Depending on your choice of topping the ideal size is between half-an-inch to one-inch squares. If your ice cubes are larger, you can easily slice the feta mousse cubes in halves as soon as you unmold them.

Cherry tomatoes. Cut the tomatoes in half and place them on a cracker with a piece of feta mouse. Drizzle with olive oil and vinegar, add a pinch of salt and finish with poppy seeds and a basil leaf.
Figs. Cut them in half and place them on a baking pan, cut side up. Drizzle 1/4 teaspoon olive oil and the same amount of balsamic vinegar on each one. Place a slice of bacon on each half fig and pop them into the oven. Bake for 10 minutes at 350°F. Let them cool completely and serve on the cracker with the feta mousse.
Watermelon. Cut nice chunks of watermelon and drizzle with salt. Put a feta mouse on a cracker and add a nice piece of watermelon. Finish with some poppy seeds.
Pears. Peel and slice the pears in half, remove the pit and add the feta mousse to the cavity of the pit. Decorate with a slice of prosciutto and some poppy seeds.

You can experiment with the feta cheese mousse. Try pairing it with a variety of vegetables and fruit with a sweet taste that contrasts with the saltiness of the feta. You will enjoy it!

Fall

Grape Tart (8-12) 🗓

This is a very tasty and interesting tart. I make it with olive oil when we have vegan students or students with dairy allergies, on their birthday, because students with dairy allergies are seldom able to enjoy a decent dessert.

150 grams or 1 1/2 cups almond powder or 1 1/4 cups blanched almonds
50 grams or 1/4 cup sugar
100 grams or 1/2 cup extra virgin olive oil (you may substitute with 1 stick of butter)
A pinch of salt
1 teaspoon pure vanilla extract
200 grams or 1 1/2 cups flour

2 cups seedless grapes of your choice
3/4 cup apricot jam or clear jello
2 tablespoons cognac or rum

1. Preheat the oven to 380°F.
2. In the food processor bowl add the almond powder and sugar and work until you reach the desired texture, resembling fine or coarse sand. I personally prefer the coarse sand texture because I love variety in textures, but this is totally up to you. Of course, if you use almond powder, which is almonds already processed to the finest texture, you do not have the choice of a coarser, more rustic dough.
3. When the almonds reach the desired texture, add the olive oil (or cold butter cut in cubes), salt, and vanilla extract and pulse until all ingredients are combined. Add the flour and pulse once or twice. Remove from the food processor and briefly work by hand until the ingredients are combined. You cannot roll out this dough because of the almond powder, so spread it by hand, as evenly as possible, into a 9-inch pie shell. If you are serving people with dairy allergies, make sure you have applied oil, instead of butter, on the pie shell. If you are using olive oil, you do not need to chill the crust. If you are using butter, chill the crust for 30

minutes. Prick with a fork several times.

4. Bake for 30-35 minutes or until the crust is golden brown. Let the crust cool completely.

5. Arrange the grapes neatly on the crust. In a small pot, warm up the apricot jam along with the cognac or rum until steam comes out. Mix well. With a pastry brush, apply all the jam to the grapes.

You can add any kind of berries you like (instead of grapes), to this tart base. It is delicious!

Robert: This is one of the best desserts I've ever had. I actually dreamed of eating it a few days after I first had it!

Cannelé (24)

These tiny little masterpieces are a French treat. I first tried one in a franchise-type bakery in France and was not impressed. When I later tried one in a good pastry shop, I fell in love. They are crunchy on the outside, almost burned at the bottom, creamy on the inside, perfectly buttery, and wonderfully aromatic. In short, small masterpieces.

With cannelé, we have to be patient and let the batter rest for two days. When we are ready to bake them, we have to create an intense heating shock, so we freeze the molds and then place them in a very, very hot oven. We have to use a specific kind of mold: the cannelé mold. But honestly, the cannelés are so worth the investment and the trouble!

50 grams or 3 1/2 tablespoons unsalted butter, plus some for the molds
500 grams or 2 cups milk, 3.5 % fat content
1 vanilla bean or 1 teaspoon vanilla extract
30 grams or 2 teaspoons dark rum
200 grams or 1 1/2 cups powdered sugar
2 eggs +2 egg yolks
100 grams or 3/4 cup flour
A pinch of salt

1. Split the vanilla bean in half, scrape the seeds, and add to the milk. In a small pot warm the butter and the milk with the vanilla bean. As soon as the butter melts, take the pot off the heat and let it cool completely. (It will not be the end of the world if you use vanilla extract, but the real vanilla bean is strongly recommended).

2. In a blender add the rum, sugar, whole eggs, egg yolks, flour, and salt, and blend just until incorporated. When the milk mixture is cool (less than 100°F), add it also, and stir briefly. Do not work the mixture more than needed.

3. Transfer the mixture to a pitcher, or large jar with a lid, through a sieve, to catch any flour lumps. Make sure to add the vanilla bean back to the pitcher as well. Store, tightly covered, in the fridge for two to five days. Stir the mixture once a day while it is stored in the fridge.

4. <u>When you are ready to bake them.</u> Preheat the oven to 470°F (I know it's hot).

5. Melt some butter and, using a pastry brush, generously butter the molds. The French use beeswax to grease the molds, but frankly, I rarely use it. I have to admit though that beeswax makes the skin of the cannelés crunchier and darker. Real butter works quite well. After you butter the molds, place them in the freezer for at least 15 minutes.

6. Place the molds on a cookie tray. Take the batter out of the fridge, stir it up, and very carefully pour it into the small, frozen molds, filling them to a little lower than the rim. Then place the cookie tray with the filled molds in the very hot oven.

7. Fifteen minutes later (if your molds are 2 inches in diameter, 10 minutes if they are smaller), turn the oven down to 350°F and open the oven door briefly to turn the cookie tray 180° (the front side will go to the back). Close the oven door fast and let them bake for 40-45 more minutes or until brown on the top. Watch them during the last 10 minutes to be sure they do not burn because at this stage they can burn really fast.

You are very welcome!

Far Breton (8-12)

A similar recipe to cannelé in ingredients is the Far Breton from Brittany, but it yields a surprisingly different result. This is an extremely comforting flan, in contrast to the stylish, fancy cannelé, yet the recipe is almost identical. How different these two desserts are is a wonderful example of how much a baking technique affects the final product.

1 cup prunes
60 grams or 1/4 cup dark rum (you could use cognac also)
50 grams or 3 1/2 tablespoons unsalted butter plus some for the dish
500 grams or 2 cups milk, 3.5% fat content
1 teaspoon pure vanilla extract
100 grams or 1/2 cup sugar
2 eggs + 2 egg yolks
100 grams or 3/4 cup flour
A pinch of salt
1 tablespoon cinnamon

1. In a small bowl add the prunes and rum and let them soak for a few hours, preferably overnight. If you do not have a few hours, while you are preparing the batter heat up the rum slightly (do not let it come to a boil) and add the prunes.
2. Preheat the oven to 400°F.
3. In a blender add the butter, melted, and the rest of the ingredients and blend until just incorporated. You can prepare this the night before and store it in the fridge overnight or even for two days, but, unlike the cannelés, you don't have to.
4. Butter a 9x11 inch, deep baking pan or a round one that is 9 or 10 inches in diameter.
5. Remove the prunes from the rum and arrange them on the bottom of the buttered pan. Add the rum to the rest of the ingredients and mix well. Carefully pour the batter over the prunes.
6. Transfer to the oven and let the flan bake for 50 minutes or until golden brown. Check for doneness by inserting a knife into the center of the dessert.
7. Let it cool slightly and dust with powdered sugar.

Tip: Cinnamon—Use Ceylon cinnamon if possible. It is more expensive than regular cinnamon but the taste is not comparable. Also, Ceylon cinnamon is a strong antioxidant and anti-inflammatory and helps regulate insulin levels. On the other hand, common, cheap cinnamon can be harmful in big doses (a tablespoon daily).

Shane: *It's like flan, but better. It's flantastic.*

Sweet Potato Chocolate Pie *(8-12)*

For one pie: Basic Crust
200 grams or 1 1/2 cups flour
1 tablespoon vinegar
1/2 teaspoon salt
120 grams or 1 stick cold, unsalted butter
2 tablespoons heavy cream
Filling
600 grams or 2 cups boiled and mashed sweet potatoes (about two medium potatoes)
120 grams or 1 stick butter, melted
A generous pinch of salt
One teaspoon cinnamon
1/8 teaspoon freshly grated nutmeg
1/4 teaspoon zest of orange peel
120 grams or 1/2 cup of fresh orange juice
2 eggs
200 grams or 1 cup brown sugar
80 grams or 1/2 cup bitter cocoa powder
120 grams or 1/2 cup unsweetened evaporated milk
Optional for serving: 1 cup heavy cream, whipped

1. Peel the sweet potatoes, cut them into chunks, and place them in a pot with cold water and two tablespoons of salt. Bring to a soft boil and let them boil until tender, around 30 minutes.
2. In the meantime, make the crust. Add the flour, vinegar, salt, and cold butter to a food processor and pulse until the butter is incorporated. Add two tablespoons of heavy cream and pulse again. If your mixture is dry, you might need to add one more tablespoon of cream until the dough holds together. Remove immediately, form into a ball, flatten it, and roll it out into a 1/4 inch thick pie crust. You will need to dust with some flour. Wrap it up with a plastic wrap, place it on a cookie sheet, and put it in the fridge for thirty minutes.
3. Heat the oven to 375°F. Take the dough out of the fridge and transfer the rolled dough into a buttered 9 inch round pie shell. Prick it several times with a fork and bake for 15 minutes.
4. Meanwhile, once the potatoes are tender, drain all the water and mash them very well. Add the butter, salt, cinnamon, nutmeg, orange zest, and orange juice while the potatoes are still hot, and let the flavors infuse as the potatoes cool down.
5. In another bowl beat the eggs with the brown sugar and, when incorporated, add the cocoa powder and milk. Add this to
 the sweet potato mixture, mix well, and taste. I love bitter chocolate so I like to add a couple more tablespoons of cocoa powder. Depending on your taste, try the mixture and decide.
6. Transfer the sweet potato mixture to the prebaked pie crust. Bake at 375°F for another 30 minutes. I like to whip up some heavy cream to serve with this rich and at the same time tangy (due to the orange juice) and flavorful pie.

Meg: This pie was AMAZING!!!!

Tip: *When making pie crust, it is advised to add your ingredients to the food processor and pulse until a sand-like consistency is achieved. Although this is an easy method to make the crust, it has a disadvantage: it processes the butter more than we want, leaving our crust without any butter flakes. To correct this, I like to save one tablespoon of butter before I place it into the food processor. I then grate it and freeze the shavings for a few minutes. As I take the crumbs out of the food processor I incorporate the frozen butter, and then roll the dough for the pie crust. This way, we end up with a flaky, perfectly buttery pie crust.*

Wine Cake (8-12)

A truly unique cake. If you make it you will fall in love with it.

150 grams or 1 stick +2 tablespoons butter, room temperature
40 grams or 2 tablespoons invert sugar (see tip) or honey
3 medium egg yolks
60 grams or 1/4 cup sweet red wine
200 grams or 1 1/2 cups flour
2 teaspoons baking powder
15 grams or 2 tablespoons unsweetened cocoa
1 tablespoon cinnamon
1/8 teaspoon ground cloves
A pinch of salt
115 grams or 4 ounces chocolate chips (I use bitter chocolate, small size chips)
3 medium egg whites
150 grams or 3/4 cup sugar

1. Turn the oven to 380°F.
2. In a bowl add the butter with 2 tablespoons of invert sugar (highly recommended) or honey and whisk at medium speed either with a handheld mixer or a stand one for 5 minutes or until the mixture turns light in color. Turn the mixer to low and add the egg yolks, one at a time, and then the wine. Whisk for a minute and turn the mixer off. The ingredients in the mixture will not be completely incorporated at this point.
3. In a bowl sift together the flour, baking powder, cocoa, cinnamon, cloves, and salt. Add the flour mixture and chocolate chips to the butter mixture. Fold until the mixture is just incorporated, but do not work the mixture more or it will thicken up too much.
4. In a clean, dry bowl add the egg whites and start whisking at medium speed. Once the mixture froths, add the sugar a tablespoon at a time. Turn the speed to high until a stiff meringue is formed. Fold 1/3 of the meringue into the cake mixture to loosen it up. Then add the rest of the meringue and fold.
5. Transfer to a buttered cake form and bake for 50 minutes or until a knife comes out clean if inserted. Unmold on a platter and dust with powdered sugar. It is irresistible if served warm.

Tip: You may substitute invert sugar with honey. Invert sugar is widely used by professional bakers because it helps the cake retain moisture better. You can keep invert sugar for months in a clean jar. For this recipe, you will need 3 tablespoons sugar + 1 tablespoon water + 1 teaspoon lemon juice, or you can make a big batch; use 200 grams of sugar (1 cup) with 100 grams water (1/2 cup) and 2 tablespoons lemon juice. Place all ingredients over medium heat. As soon as the syrup starts to boil, lower the heat so that it is barely simmering. Let it simmer for 15 minutes and take it off the heat before it turns amber. We need it to stay white or slightly yellow. If you are making only 3 tablespoons of sugar, take it off the heat as soon as it starts to boil because the liquid evaporates fast.

Alex: *Thanksgiving packed in a slice of cake.*

Cinnamon Rolls, different (10-12)

I am not exactly sure what to name this dessert: cinnamon roll, apple pie, coffee cake... it has an element of each. What I do know though is that it is very tasty.

Dough
140 grams or 1/2 cup +2 tablespoons milk
100 grams or 1/2 cup sugar
1 package dry yeast
2 eggs
Zest of one lemon
1/2 teaspoon vanilla extract
400 grams or 3 cups bread flour
A pinch of salt
60 grams or 1/2 stick unsalted butter, soft not melted

Filling and Topping
120 grams or 1 stick unsalted butter, room temperature
125 grams or 1 cup flour (all-purpose flour)
A pinch of salt
1/2 teaspoon vanilla extract
100 grams or 1/2 cup brown sugar, lightly packed
55 grams or 1/2 cup almond powder
3 tablespoons cinnamon
1 big apple or two medium ones

1. Warm the milk with the sugar slightly (80°F), take off the heat and add the yeast. Stir until all the yeast dissolves. Transfer to a mixer bowl and add the eggs, lemon zest, vanilla, and half of the flour. We always use bread flour (or strong flour) with yeast so that our dough creates strong gluten connections and rises well. Mix until the flour is incorporated and add the rest of the flour and salt. Work the mixture with a kneading hook at a very slow speed for five minutes and then start adding the butter, a little at a time, until it is all incorporated and the dough is soft and elastic. Cover with plastic wrap and let it rise for at least 30 minutes.

2. In the meantime make the topping: place the butter, flour, salt, and vanilla in the bowl of the food processor and work until all are incorporated and resemble a sandy mixture. Add the sugar and almond powder slowly until just incorporated. Do not overwork the mixture. Take a cup of the mixture and save it in the fridge, covered.

3. Roll out the risen yeast dough to a rectangle. Sprinkle the topping (minus the one cup you placed in the fridge) as evenly as possible. Peel your apple and cut it in small cubes, about half an inch squares. Spread on the dough evenly. Roll up your dough as tightly as possible and cut it into 10 or 12 rolls. Place the rolls in a buttered pan and let them rise for 30 minutes.

4. Preheat the oven to 380°F.

5. Sprinkle the topping you saved onto your cinnamon rolls and place the pan in the oven. Bake the rolls for 35-40 minutes until they get a nice golden color.

Tip: *You may use this dough to make regular cinnamon rolls. Alternatively, you may use it in a cake form and add pieces of fruit to it. Use fruit that does not produce a lot of moisture, like apples, pears, figs, or apricots, to make a very tasty cake. Cut the fruit into wedges and place them in the dough before you bake it. Finish with the same topping for a very tasty and crunchy element.*

Pudding with Sabayon

When I make the Cinnamon Rolls recipe (the previous one), I double the amount of the dough to make sure that I have leftover rolls to make pudding after the rolls dry out. You could also use a dried cake, brioche, or even plain toast bread to make the pudding, but the final taste is not going to be the same. At any rate, whatever you use, you need to adjust the ingredients accordingly. For example, if you make the pudding with plain bread, you need to replace all the milk with cream and add some more sugar. Use your judgment in this.

Cut your cake into small pieces and measure it by filling a cup but not squeezing the crumbs into it. Use a pan that is big enough for the amount of dry cake you have. For every cup of dried cake or brioche, you will need:

1 cup of milk or cream (for one cup of dried cake**)**
1 egg
2 tablespoons sugar
1 teaspoon dark rum
1/3 teaspoon pure vanilla extract
1 tablespoon raisins
1 tablespoon white chocolate chips
A handful of chopped almonds
1/2 teaspoon cinnamon
A pinch of salt
(after the first three ingredients, the rest are optional)

Paige: Natasa's French pudding: I am stunned

1. Butter a ceramic dish and add the dried cake or brioche to it. Add the raisins, chocolate chips, almonds, cinnamon and salt and mix well so that they are distributed evenly between the cake crumbs.

2. In another bowl beat the eggs, add the milk or cream and incorporate completely. Add the sugar, rum, vanilla, and whisk. Pour over the cake and let it soak for at least 30 minutes or even overnight (it makes an excellent brunch dish).

3. When you are ready to serve, turn the oven to 380°F. Bake the pudding for 30 minutes or until the top is nicely golden and firm if you pinch it. Serve hot with some irresistible Sabayon.

Sabayon
3 egg yolks
3 tablespoon sugar
3 tablespoons rum or Masala
1/3 cup heavy cream

In a bowl add the egg yolks, sugar, and mix. Place the bowl over a pot with water (Bain Marie) that is gently simmering. Start whisking with an electric mixer, add the rum and continue until the mixture starts to thicken and the temperature (if you check with a food thermometer) reaches 160°F. The more you whisk, the thicker it will get, so stop when your cream reaches the desired consistency. In another bowl whisk the heavy cream to a soft peak consistency and gently fold it into the egg cream. Enjoy it over your pudding.

Tip: Eggs. Europeans keep their eggs outside the fridge for two or three weeks. They keep perfectly fine and fresh. In Greece, we only place our eggs in the fridge during the hot summer months.

Almond Cookies: Amygdalota (24) 🍴 🌾

Amigdalota is literally translated Almondy. There are two versions of the Almond Cookies: a fluffy cookie that is like a macaron, and a dense one that is made mostly on the Greek islands. My grandmother was from the island of Poros where this cookie is a specialty. When we were kids, we would ride the ferry to visit Poros, and as the ferry turned to get into the port of Poros, the famous clock tower of the island on top of the hill would appear in front of us with the beautiful, blue, glittering dome in all its glory, hanging over the white island houses. It seemed to me that the shape of this beautiful dome was the prototype for the almond treats. As soon as I could see the dome, my mouth would water for this gem…

160 grams or 6 ounces blanched almonds or 1 1/2 cups almond powder
100 grams or 1/2 cup sugar
3 tablespoons bread crumbs (you may skip these if you are gluten intolerant)
2 tablespoons flower water (in delicatessen stores) **OR orange zest + cinnamon**
1 egg white
1 cup powdered sugar for dusting

1. Place the almonds, sugar, salt, and bread crumbs in a food processor and work it until the mixture resembles a sandy texture. Add the egg white and one tablespoon flower water. If you do not like flower water (or you do not have some), you can use the zest of half an orange and a teaspoon of cinnamon for flavoring. Pulse a few times until the mixture becomes homogeneous. If you skip the breadcrumbs the cookies might crack easier, but the taste will not be affected.

2. Turn the oven to 340°F and line a cookie sheet with parchment paper.

3. Form the Amygdalota into football-shaped balls (one end will flatten when you place it on the cookie sheet) and place them on the cookie sheet, standing upright.

3. Bake for 15-20 minutes (depending on the size) until their bottoms become light golden.

4. Take them out of the oven and sprinkle some more flower water on them with your fingers. Let them cool completely and then roll them in powdered sugar.

The other version is basically made with the same ingredients (minus the flower water plus 2 egg whites) but with a different technique, resulting in a different form. You have to whisk three egg whites with a pinch of salt and sugar into a stiff meringue and fold the almonds (processed into a very fine powder) and the bread crumbs into the meringue. Proceed by shaping the cookies like the Hazelnut cookies (next recipe) with a piping bag. Bake them at 340°F for 15-20 minutes (until their bottom is dry and does not stick to the parchment paper). Let them cool and apply the marmalade of your choice on half of the cookies and then cover each one with a plain one, like a macaron. If you are allergic to gluten, skip the breadcrumbs.

Hazelnut cookies *(24)* 🗆 🗆

These cookies are made with hazelnuts and are great with a chocolate sauce called ganache. You could make them with walnuts, also.

200 grams or 7 ounces hazelnuts
3 tablespoons or 1 ounce bread crumbs (you may skip that if you are gluten intolerant. Cookies might not keep their shape as well, but the taste will not be compromised)
1 teaspoon cinnamon
1/4 teaspoon ground cloves
3 egg whites
200 grams or 1 cup sugar
A pinch of salt

Filling: Ganache
80 grams or 1/3 cup cream
120 grams or 4 ounces dark chocolate
A pinch of salt

1. Turn the oven on to 340°F.
2. In a food processor, add the hazelnuts, bread crumbs, cinnamon, and cloves, and work the mixture until its texture becomes like fine sand.
3. In a clean and dry mixer bowl, add the egg whites and turn the mixer on medium. Once the eggs start to froth, add the sugar, one tablespoon at a time. When all the sugar is added, turn the mixer speed up to high. Whisk until a very thick meringue is formed. (If you lift the whisk, the peak is barely leaning over).
4. Turn the mixer off and fold in the hazelnut mixture in two batches. Be careful not to overwork the mixture: we don't want to lose all the air of the meringue, but you do not have to be fearful either. Use big and steady movements with your spatula in your right hand, while at the same time turning the bowl counterclockwise with your left one.
5. Once all the ingredients are incorporated, transfer the mixture to a piping bag with a star tip and form discs that are as consistent in size as possible. I usually make them around 2 inches in diameter.
6. Bake for 15 minutes, turn the oven off, and let them cool in the oven for 15 more minutes before you take them out.
7. In a small pot, heat the cream until it steams but does not come to a boil. Transfer the hot cream to a bowl in which you have already placed the chocolate, chopped into small pieces.
8. Let the chocolate stand for two minutes in the cream to soften and then mix with a spatula until it is all melted and the sauce looks smooth and silky. Add a pinch of salt and mix. Let the ganache (that is the name of the chocolate sauce) cool down completely while the cookies are also cooling down. The ganache sauce will get thicker as time passes.
9. When completely cool transfer the ganache to a piping bag and place a walnut-size drop on half of the cookies. Cover them with the other halves and create small delicious sandwiches.

Liann: French Macarons have nothing on these Greek beauties!

Baklava (24) 🍶

There are countless ways, recipes, and combinations for making baklava. You can use any nut you like with any flavoring you prefer. I love pistachio so I will give you my favorite recipe for a pistachio baklava. You have to be very careful with the phyllo dough; since it contains no fat, it will dry very fast. Get everything ready before opening the dough package. After you open the package, cover it with a damp kitchen towel. If you have dairy allergies, make baklava with olive oil. Greeks make baklava with olive oil during Lent.

1 package of phyllo dough. Let it thaw in the fridge for at least two hours (and up to five or six days), and then let it come to room temperature on the counter.

1/2 cup unsalted, melted butter or olive oil

Filling

500 grams or 1 pound unsalted pistachios

100 grams or 1/2 cup sugar

Vanilla extract

1/4 teaspoon salt

Zest of one orange (optional)

Syrup

200 grams or 1 cup water

200 grams or 1 cup sugar

Zest and juice of an orange

1. Turn the oven to 380°F. In a small pot prepare the syrup. Mix the water, sugar, orange zest, and orange juice, bring to a boil, and let the syrup boil for five minutes. Remove from the heat and let it cool. In another pot melt the butter.

2. Prepare the filling. In a food processor, add all the filling ingredients and pulse for a few seconds at a time until you have a coarse sand-like consistency,

3. Open the phyllo dough package and lay it flat before you. Choose a pan with a similar length to that of the phyllo so that the phyllo fits well in it. If the pan is smaller than your phyllo, lay the pan on top of the phyllo stack and cut off the area of the phyllo that is too big. Butter the pan with the melted butter or olive oil. Take the top phyllo sheet and lay it flat in the pan. Butter the phyllo. Repeat with four phyllo sheets, laying them flat in the pan and buttering each one. This is our base.

4. After you butter the fourth phyllo, spread 6-7 generous tablespoons of the filling. Continue by layering one phyllo, buttering it and spreading 6 tablespoons of the filling, until all the filling is spent. You should be left with some more phyllos.

5. Layer and butter the rest of the phyllo sheets, one by one, until they are finished.

6. Butter the top phyllo and then sprinkle a little water on it for crunchiness. With a very sharp knife, cut the baklava into small squares. Cut carefully through the bottom.

7. Bake in the oven for 30 minutes until it starts to become golden. Take the baklava out of the oven, and very carefully drench it with the syrup. Return the baklava to the oven for 5-10 more minutes until golden brown. Let it cool completely before you serve it. You do not have to consume the baklava immediately because it actually gets better with time. Save some and eat it two or three weeks later. You'll thank me.

Caroline: *I remember shoving baklava in my mouth the night before we left Greece…*
(Caroline's group left Greece abruptly a day after COVID-19 was declared a pandemic).

Saragli (24) 🖾

Saragli is cylindrical baklava, one of many variations. What sets saragli apart and makes it interesting is that the saragli is wrapped around a rod, cut, and then baked, producing a gap in the middle which results in airy, crunchy baklava. I am going to give you an alternative filling recipe with walnuts, or you may use the previous recipe with pistachio. You will need a clean rod, wooden or metal, that is at least 15 inches long and around 1/2 inch in diameter.

1 package of phyllo dough. Let it thaw in the fridge for at least two hours or on the counter for 30 minutes
1/2 cup unsalted, melted butter or olive oil (we use olive oil during the Lent season)

Filling
500 grams or 1 pound walnuts
100 grams or 1/2 cup sugar
1 teaspoon cinnamon
1/8 teaspoon ground cloves
1/4 teaspoon salt

Syrup
200 grams or 1 cup water
200 grams or 1 cup sugar
Zest of an orange
Juice of half an orange

1. Turn the oven to 380°F. In a small pot melt the butter. Butter a 9x12 inch pan. In another pot prepare the syrup. Mix the water, sugar, orange zest, and juice and boil for five minutes. Remove from the heat and let it cool.
2. Prepare the filling. In a food processor, add all the filling ingredients and pulse a few times until you have a sand-like consistency.
3. Open the phyllo dough package and lay it flat with the long side towards you. Brush the top phyllo sheet with butter or olive oil. Sprinkle four tablespoons of the filling on the phyllo, leaving one inch without filling at both short ends. Take the rod, place it along one of the short sides of the phyllo (perpendicular to you) and wrap the phyllo on the rod. Push the two ends of the phyllo towards the center, creating a shorter "pleated" cylindrical baklava. Take a sharp knife and cut the baklava in two places, going around the rod to create three equal pieces. If you try to cut the saragli in the pan, you will cause the collapse of the air gap which we went through all this trouble to create. Place the 3 saraglis in the pan and proceed with the next phyllo.
4. When all the filling is used, butter the top of the saraglis carefully and take the pan to the oven. Bake for 30 minutes until the top starts to brown. Take the pan out of the oven, and very carefully drench the saraglis with the syrup. Return to the oven for 5-10 more minutes or until golden brown. Let it cool completely before you serve it.

Mac: I should not have had this baklava at the beginning of my trip to Greece... it ruined all other baklavas for the rest of my time there.

Killaj with pistachio and Ricotta (24)

A unique, tasty, and elegant dessert from Lebanon. It looks more complicated than it is. At any rate, you can simplify the way you roll the phyllo dough. You may even give the killaj the shape of a spring roll. I promise they will be just as tasty, even if they look less exotic.

1 package phyllo dough, thawed
120 grams or 1 stick butter
200 grams or 7 ounces pistachio
A pinch of salt
200 grams or 7 ounces ricotta
150 grams or 3/4 cup sugar
45 grams or 1/3 cup flour
1/2 teaspoon baking powder
Zest of half orange
Syrup
200 grams or 1 cup water
300 grams or 1 1/2 cups sugar
Juice of 1 orange
Zest of half an orange

1. Make the syrup. Wash an orange and zest it. Add half of the zest to a small pot (save the rest for later) along with the water, sugar, and juice of the orange and bring to a boil. Let it boil for 5 minutes, and set it aside to cool down. In another pot melt the butter.

2. In a food processor, add the pistachios and salt and grind until you have the consistency of fine sand. Add the zest of the half orange you saved earlier. Transfer to another bowl.

3. In the empty food processor add the ricotta cheese and sugar and pulse briefly. Add the flour, and baking powder and pulse again, just until incorporated. Transfer the mixture to a piping bag with a medium round tip (#12 if you are using Wilton).

4. Turn the oven to 380°F. Butter a 10x13 inch pan.

5. Open the dough package and remove one phyllo sheet. Place it flat in front of you. With your fingers "pleat" the middle portion of the phyllo, leaving an inch to the left and an inch to the right, as shown in the picture.

6. Visualize your killaj: you will cut the dough every three inches. Place 1 teaspoon of pistachios 1.5 inches from the top end. Leave a three inches gap and place another teaspoon. Continue placing 1 teaspoon every three inches until you reach the bottom of the phyllo.

7. Place a walnut-size cheese filling on every pistachio hump. When you are done with this phyllo, use a glass of water to wet your fingers, and wet the two parallel flat ends of the phyllo, and then the gaps in between the filling, creating Hs. Turn one long end of the phyllo on the filling and then turn the other long end on top of the first. Pinch the gaps in between the pistachio cheese filling, where you applied water, to seal the killaj.

8. With a sharp knife cut the phyllo in the middle of the empty gaps, where you pinched the dough. Squeeze the two ends of each killaj and, with both hands, lift it and flip it upside down. Place it on the buttered pan, squeezing it close to the previous one.

9. Now is the time to generously apply butter to the formed killaj. We want the butter to go into every little crease if possible.

10. When you are done buttering the top of the pastries, take your pan to the oven and bake for twenty minutes. Take it out of the oven and pour the syrup carefully over each killaj. Return the pan to the oven for another 10-15 minutes. Let the killaj cool slightly before you dig into them. They are unique, very tasty and so worth the trouble of making!

Tip: A favorite filling with our students (NOT typically Greek) is peanut butter, especially when students with tree nut allergies are here. I spread some peanut butter on a phyllo sheet and add chocolate chips or M&Ms. I then roll the phyllo, bake it partially, add the syrup and bake it for ten more minutes, just as we do with the regular baklava.

Jenna: I remember you making some amazing baklava with peanut butter and chocolate chips! It was such a fun twist on the Greek dessert!
Courtney: When you made the baklava with M&Ms and peanut butter, I had to keep going back and stealing little pieces. It was so good, I still think about that dessert to this day!

Custard Pie or Galaktoboureko *(8-12)*

A lemony, creamy custard between two sets of crunchy phyllo dough, with lemony syrup…

1 package of phyllo dough, thawed
120 grams or 1 stick melted butter
Custard
1 liter or 4 cups milk 3.5% fat content
100 grams or 1/2 cup sugar
90 grams or 1/2 cup fine semolina or regular cream of wheat (not instant)
1 teaspoon pure vanilla extract
45 grams or 3 tablespoons butter
Zest of 1 lemon
2 eggs
Syrup
150 grams or 3/4 cup water
200 grams or 1 cup sugar
1 tablespoon lemon juice and zest of one lemon

1. Make the syrup first. Place all syrup ingredients in a small pot and bring to a boil. Let the syrup boil for five minutes, take it off the heat, and let it cool. Preheat the oven to 350°F.
2. In a small pot melt 1 stick of butter and set it aside. Place the milk, sugar and semolina in another pot. Mix well and then turn the heat on medium-high. Stir constantly until the cream starts to thicken. When it is thick enough to coat the back of the spoon, take it off the heat. Add the vanilla extract, 3 TB butter, lemon zest, and two beaten eggs, whisking vigorously until all incorporated. Cover with plastic wrap directly on the surface and let the cream cool.
3. Open the phyllo package and count the sheets of the phyllo dough. You will place more phyllo on the bottom than the top with the cream in between. E.g, if you have 12 sheets of phyllo, place 7 on the bottom and 5 on top. Choose a pan that works well with the size of your phyllo. The pan should be slightly smaller than your phyllo. Usually, 9x11 works well. There should be enough phyllo to cover the bottom and come up the sides of the pan just a bit. If your pan is bigger, you can adjust by not aligning every phyllo exactly with the previous one, creating full coverage. Place the first phyllo on a buttered pan. Butter it well with the melted butter. Place another phyllo on top, butter it and continue, layering and buttering all bottom layers of phyllo. This is the base.
4. Carefully transfer the cream onto the last base phyllo and level it. Place another phyllo on top of the cream, butter it and continue until you finish all your phyllos. Proceed by bringing the overhanging parts of the side phyllos in, folding them on themselves to seal the cream in.
5. Butter the top and the edges generously. Dip your fingers in water and sprinkle some on top. With a sharp knife, score the top phyllo in squares or in diagonal lines.
6. Transfer the pan with the custard pie to the oven and bake for 40-45 minutes until the phyllos are golden brown and the cream is set.
7. Take the custard pie out of the oven and while still very hot, drizzle the cool syrup on top of the pie. Let it set for 20 minutes before you cut it. It's irresistible when still warm.

Natasa: I made this for the first group of students I cooked for and told them it was milk pie (which is the accurate translation from Greek) and they didn't even try it. I was devastated. A couple of weeks later I made it again and told them it was "custard pie". They LOVED "custard pie"!

Koliva (12-16) 🍶

This is a preparation with a heavy mythological burden that revolves around death, as it is associated with the myth of Persephone who stole seven pomegranate seeds from Hades, the god of the dead. Demeter, the mother of Persephone is the goddess of harvest who taught mankind the art of agriculture. The myth itself is very interesting and explains in a fascinating way the circle of death and rebirth of nature.

Unfortunately, a nutritional treasure like this is lost in the weight of its mythological connotations.

500 grams or 1 pound of wheat (uncracked)

110 grams or 1/2 cup brown sugar

2 cups nuts of your choice (almonds, walnuts, and hazelnuts are used traditionally)

1 tablespoon cinnamon

1/4 teaspoon ground cloves

Pomegranate seeds, berries, raisins, and/or dried figs

1. Wash the uncracked wheat and place it in plenty of water in a pot. Add a pinch of salt and bring to a gentle boil. We need to simmer the wheat for 40-50 minutes until it is soft but does not break open.

2. Drain the wheat but save the water to be used for our next dessert. Spread the boiled wheat between two kitchen towels to absorb as much moisture as possible. Leave for at least 30 minutes. If you have time, refrigerate overnight, covered with a towel.

3. In a saucepan toast the nuts (almonds, walnuts, hazelnuts) slightly to enhance their taste. Chop the dried figs (if you are using some) very fine and the nuts into big chunks.

4. Mix all ingredients and serve. You may keep the koliva for a few days in the fridge.

Assure (8-10)

5 cups of the water the wheat boiled in from the previous recipe
80 grams or 1/2 cup cornstarch
1 cup of boiled wheat
100 - 200 grams or ½ -1 cup sugar (it is up to you how sour or sweet you want it)
1/2 cup of dried fruit cut into small pieces (raisins, apricots, figs)
1/2 cup of chopped nuts (walnuts, almonds, pistachios, or a combination)
1 tablespoon cinnamon
1/4 teaspoon ground cloves
Pomegranate seeds and/or berries for decoration

1. Take out 5 cups of the water the wheat boiled in (you may add more water during boiling).
2. Add the water to a pot along with the cornstarch and mix well. It is very important that the cornstarch is dissolved in cold water, so if the water you boiled the wheat in, is still warm, dissolve the cornstarch in a cup of cold water first. After you dissolve the cornstarch, add the boiled wheat and the sugar and turn the heat on to medium. If you add half a cup of sugar your Assure will not be sweet but will have a delicate sour aftertaste. If you prefer to have a sweet cream, add one cup of sugar. Cook for a few minutes, while stirring constantly, until the mixture starts to thicken, turns translucent, and bubbles up. You may notice that here we use 5 cups of liquid with 1/2 cup of cornstarch instead of the 4 cups of liquid we used in previous recipes (page 66). We do this because there is already some starch in the water we boiled the wheat in.
3. As soon as the mixture bubbles, add the rest of the ingredients. Mix and then remove from the heat. Serve in individual glasses and refrigerate. It is delicious and very healthy. Decorate with nuts, pomegranate seeds and berries.

Pistachio or Almond Brittle (20) 🌾

Our students love brittle. They just cannot get enough. If you have tree nut allergies but can eat peanuts, make brittle with peanuts. It is still very good.

100 grams or 1/2 cup minus one tablespoon of heavy cream
100 grams or 1/2 cup sugar
40 grams or 2 tablespoons honey
120 grams or 4 ounces pistachios or almonds
1/2 teaspoon sea salt

1. Preheat the oven to 330°F.
2. Chop the nuts roughly. You may use either kind of nut or a combination. Add the salt and mix.
3. In a small pot, add the cream, sugar, and honey and stir to combine. Turn the heat on to medium. Let the mixture reach 245°F. If you do not have a candy thermometer, let the mixture come to a boil, wait for three or four minutes and with a spoon take a few drops and let them drip in a glass of cold water. The mixture is ready when the drop reaches the bottom of the glass unchanged and has not dissolved in the water. Also, there is going to be a thread forming when the drops fall. Take the mixture off the heat immediately.
4. Add the salted nuts to the mixture and stir until combined. If you have a macaron silicon form, it is perfect to use it. Take one tablespoon of the mixture, drop it in the macaron form, spread it, and continue until all the brittle mixture is used. If you do not have a macaron form, spread the brittle mixture on parchment paper that you have placed on a cookie sheet. Spread the brittle scoops so that there is a thin layer of nuts.
5. Take the brittle to the oven and bake for 18-20 minutes or until they start to turn darker.
6. If you have used a macaron form, just wait for the brittle to cool and unmold them. Otherwise, when you take them out of the oven, let them cool for ten minutes. Butter a sharp knife and cut the cookies into 1x1 inch squares or triangles. Let them cool completely before you handle them.

Tip: If your brittle is not as crunchy as you wanted (after they cool down), take them back to the oven and bake for a few more minutes until their color darkens a little further.

Jessica: Pistachio brittle!!! I remember thinking how I needed it every day of my life. I still have not found anything even remotely close, and I crave it all the time!

Nougatine: Dacquoise with Cream (12)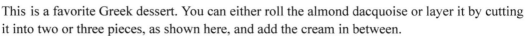

This is a favorite Greek dessert. You can either roll the almond dacquoise or layer it by cutting it into two or three pieces, as shown here, and add the cream in between.

Base: Almond Dacquoise

4 egg whites
A pinch of salt
50 grams or 1/4 cup sugar
125 grams or 1 cup powdered sugar
100 grams or 1 cup almond powder
1 teaspoon flour or cornstarch for pan

Diplomat Cream

480 grams or 2 cups milk
240 grams or 1 cup cream
½ vanilla bean
100 grams or 1/2 cup sugar
40 grams or 1/2 cup cornstarch
4 egg yolks
1 whole egg
1/2 teaspoon almond extract (optional, but highly recommended)
180 grams or 3/4 cup heavy cream, whipped
Decoration: 1/2 cup almonds chopped and 1 cup sugar (to make caramel)

1. Turn the oven to 330°F. Take a cookie sheet and line it with parchment paper. Butter the paper lightly and sprinkle with 1 teaspoon flour (or you may use cornstarch if there is a gluten allergy). Shake to remove any extra and set pan aside.

2. In the mixer bowl, add the 4 egg whites and start whisking at medium. When the mixture froths, add the salt and sugar, one tablespoon at a time, and then the powdered sugar. As soon as all the sugar is incorporated, turn the mixer speed to medium-high and continue whisking.

3. When the meringue thickens up to stiff peaks, turn the mixer off and fold in the almond powder. Spread the mixture evenly on the parchment paper in a rectangular form either with a spatula or a piping bag. Place in oven and bake for 25-30 minutes. If the dacquoise does not come off the paper easily, turn the oven off and leave the dacquoise in it to dry for another 10 minutes. Take it out of the oven and flip it on another parchment paper. Peel the paper you baked it on but let the dacquoise cool covered with this paper.

4. In a pot warm the milk, cream, and half the vanilla bean and seeds (scrape the seeds off first). I would urge you to use a vanilla bean and not vanilla extract for this dessert.

5. In a bowl whisk the sugar, cornstarch, 4 egg yolks, and egg. As soon as the milk starts to steam, take a ladle of the milk and add it to the egg yolks. Mix and add a second ladleful and then a third, mixing very well each time. Transfer the egg yolk mixture to the pot with the rest of the milk and stir vigorously for 20 seconds. Turn the heat to low and continue stirring. As soon as the mixture bubbles up, take it off the heat and transfer it to a clean bowl. Cover with plastic wrap directly on top of the cream. Place the bowl over an ice water bath.

6. Place the cream in the fridge to cool and set for about an hour. When the cream is cool,

transfer to a mixer bowl, add 3/4 cup heavy cream and the almond extract (if you are using it) and whisk the cream until thick. This is called diplomat cream.

7. When the dacquoise and the cream are cool, assemble the dessert. Save one cup of the cream and apply the rest as evenly as possible on the dacquoise. Wait for 2-3 minutes for the dacquoise to gain moisture and then roll it tightly with the help of the parchment paper. Decorate with the saved cream. Add chopped almonds and broken caramel to garnish.

Caramel: In a heavy saucepan add the sugar over medium heat. Let it melt, swirling the pan to mix the caramel until it takes an amber color. If it starts to darken, control the temperature by lifting the pan off the heat for a few seconds. When completely melted pour the caramel over the parchment paper that you have spread on the kitchen counter. Let it cool completely before you break the caramel (see page 8 on caramel making).

Shane: I took a bite and I knew my life would never be the same…
Bailey: can you make this at my wedding, please?

Kiunafe (8)

Not your average cheese pie….I think this dessert should come with a warning, "highly addictive." It is a very common treat in Middle Eastern cultures and when I first tried Kiunafe I was honestly dreaming about it for weeks.

It is made with Kataifi phyllo which is a shredded-looking dough. It produces very tasty desserts because it absorbs butter and syrup very well. You will find it frozen in Middle Eastern Markets or in big supermarkets, especially around Christmas, or you can order it online.

1 package of kataifi dough
200 grams or 1 1/2 sticks butter
300 grams or 10 ounces of cream cheese
2 tablespoons water
150 grams or 5 ounces fresh mozzarella
Syrup
300 grams or 1 1/2 cups sugar
300 grams or 1 1/2 cups water
Zest and juice of an orange
1/2 cup pistachios for decoration

1. Melt the butter and let it cool slightly. Turn the oven on at 400°F.

2. Let the kataifi dough thaw completely. Generously butter a round 9-inch pan. Open the kataifi package and spread half of it in the pan, rubbing it between your palms so that no strings are stuck together. Drizzle with half of the butter.

3. In a bowl combine the cream cheese with the water until smooth. Do not stir hard because the mixture will thicken. We want the opposite: to loosen the mixture so that we can spread it on the dough. After you spread the cream cheese mixture as evenly as possible, spread the mozzarella on top. Make sure your mozzarella is fresh, not the dry version we use on pizzas.

4. Arrange the rest of the kataifi on top of the cheeses, again rubbing between your palms to separate. Drizzle with the rest of the butter as evenly as possible. With your palms or with a plate, push the kataifi dough down so that there are no loose threads and take it to the oven.

5. While it bakes, place all the syrup ingredients into a pot and bring them to a boil. Five minutes later, turn the heat off.

6. Twenty-five minutes after you place the kiunafe in the oven it should start to take a golden color. Take it out of the oven and slowly drizzle with the syrup, as evenly as possible. Return to the oven for another ten or fifteen minutes, until golden brown. Make sure that the bottom of the kiunafe is well baked. Readjust the setting of your oven, if needed, (most ovens have a setting for bottom heat) to ensure a well-baked bottom, or cover the top with aluminum foil during the last ten minutes.

7. Take out of the oven, unmold it upside down on a platter, and decorate with chopped pistachios. Serve hot.

Nikias: I got some leftovers home and ate a spoonful for breakfast, every morning....worth its weight in gold!

(Hand Modeling: Gracelyn, Kennedy, Laura, Layne, Madgalene, Makenna, Savannah)

Cranberry Pie (8-12) 📖

I love cranberries and I was trying to figure out a way to incorporate them into a pie. I thought this pie would be good, but I didn't expect it to be *that* good...

Pie Crust
200 grams or 1 1/2 cups flour
1/2 teaspoon salt
15 grams or a tablespoon of sugar
120 grams or 1 stick butter (cold) **OR**
1/3 cup olive oil (dairy-free version)
2 tablespoons cold water
Filling
200 grams or 1 cup sugar
55 grams or 4 tablespoons brown sugar
1/2 teaspoon salt
Zest of one orange
320 grams or 1 cup corn syrup
1 teaspoon vanilla extract
90 grams or 3/4 of a stick of butter, melted
3 eggs

1 1/2 cups fresh cranberries or frozen, not dry
1/2 cup chopped pistachios or pecans (Optional. Do not use if you have a nut allergy**)**

1. Place the flour, salt, and sugar in a food processor and mix. Add the cold butter, cut in cubes, or use olive oil (for a dairy-free dessert) and pulse a few times until a sand-like texture is created. Add two tablespoons of cold water and pulse again. Check if the dough holds together. It might need a few more drops of water. As soon as it holds together, take the dough out of the food processor and press it together to form a ball. Dust with flour to facilitate the rolling. Roll it out, between two parchment papers, into a 1/4 inch thick crust. Place it in the fridge, wrapped in parchment paper or plastic wrap, for at least 30 minutes.

2. Turn the oven to 390°F. In a small pot melt the butter (¾ of a stick) and set it aside to cool.

3. Place the sugar, brown sugar, salt, and orange zest in a bowl and mix. Add the corn syrup, vanilla, and melted butter (make sure it has cooled down to lukewarm) and whisk until all is incorporated. Finally, add the eggs and whisk again.

4. Butter a 9-inch pie dish and transfer the dough into the dish. Carefully trim the edges so they are neatly cut.

5. Add the filling mixture to the unbaked pie crust. Place the fresh cranberries on top and sprinkle with the chopped pistachios or pecans. Take the pie to the oven. If you are using frozen cranberries make sure to let them thaw on paper towels before you use them.

6. Bake for 55-60 minutes until the filling is set and the dough edge has taken a golden brown color. Let it cool down and serve.

Liann: An exciting new take on tradition. What a smart idea for an incredible pie!

Apple Crostata (8) ☐

You may use butter or olive oil for the crust if there is a dairy allergy in the family. I believe you will find the combination of baked apples and tahini sauce simply exquisite. It is also very healthy, packed with antioxidants, vitamins, and minerals.

Crust

300 grams or 2 1/4 cups flour
80 grams or 6 tablespoons sugar
A pinch of salt
180 grams or 1 1/2 stick cold butter, cut into cubes
2 tablespoons ice-cold water

Filling

3 medium apples (I usually get Pink Lady but any red would do)
5 tablespoons tahini sauce
3 tablespoons honey
1 teaspoon cinnamon
1 teaspoon cognac or Grand Marnie liqueur (optional)
1/2 cup of walnuts or almonds roughly chopped (optional)
1/4 cup apricot jam

1. Start by making the crust. In a food processor add the flour, sugar, salt, and butter (or olive oil, if you prefer a dairy-free dessert) and pulse until the texture resembles coarse sand. Add a tablespoon of cold water and pulse again. Add the second tablespoon and pulse briefly. Check that the dough holds together or add a few more drops of water. Form into a ball and then flatten it to the shape of a disc. Cover it with plastic wrap or place it in a big zip lock bag. Place in the fridge for at least 30 minutes.

2. Turn the oven on at 380°F.

3. Wash the apples thoroughly and cut them in half. Remove the stem and core and, with a mandoline, slice the apples at 1/6 of an inch thickness (thinner than 1/4, thicker than 1/8). As you are slicing the apples, stack them neatly on a plate.

4. Take the dough out of the fridge and roll it out to about 14 inches in diameter. It is easier to roll it between two parchment papers or sil pats. Place the dough in a round, 12-inch pan or on parchment paper on a cookie sheet. Arrange half of the apple slices on the crust, leaving a one or two inches ring around the edge without any apples.

5. Mix the tahini sauce with honey, cinnamon, and cognac until incorporated. The more you mix, the thicker it will become. Mix until your mixture is thick enough to stay on the apples. Apply the tahini honey sauce onto the apples as evenly as possible.

6. Arrange neatly the rest of the apples on the tahini and honey sauce. If you want to add the chopped walnuts or almonds, add them on top of the final layer of apples. Fold the one-inch wide dough, that we have left without filling, onto the apples.

7. Bake for 45-50 minutes or until the dough looks golden brown. Ten minutes before you take the pie out of the oven, brush the apples with the apricot jam (if your jam is thick, warm it up first) and cover the top with parchment paper so that the apples and the top dough do not get too dark while the bottom is still cooking. Serve plain or with vanilla ice cream.

Brooklyn: *Tahini and honey sauce is one of my favorite things to eat.*
Paired with apples is simply amazing!

Savory Crostata: beet and feta cheese (8)

Crostadas are wonderful pies that can be made with a variety of vegetables. Alterenatevely, this one can be made with zucchini or squash instead of beets. You may also use any cheese you like instead of feta cheese or in combination with feta. Experiment to find your favorite.

You may use butter as in the previous Crostata, or you may use extra virgin olive oil for a lighter version, especially if one of your guests has a dairy allergy. It is very tasty and very healthy. The only problem is that an olive oil dough is crumbly so your crostata might look more rustic. For the sake of the picture, I used butter in this one.

<u>Crust</u>
200 grams or 1 1/2 cups flour
A pinch of salt
1 teaspoon baking powder
1/4 teaspoon of orange zest
1 egg yolk
2 tablespoons cold water
100 grams or 1/2 cup olive oil (or 1 stick butter)

5 medium beets
2 tablespoons olive oil
1 tablespoon red wine vinegar
1 clove garlic, crushed
1/4 teaspoon thyme
A pinch of salt
150 grams or 5 ounces feta cheese
1/2 cup walnuts (optional)

1. In a food processor add all crust ingredients except from the olive oil and pulse until incorporated. Start adding the olive oil slowly until the dough holds together. You may need less olive oil than half cup. Place in a zip lock bag or wrap in plastic or parchment paper and place in the fridge for thirty minutes.

2. Place the beets in cold water and bring them to a boil. Once the water starts to boil, mark ten minutes and take them out. When they are cool enough to handle, peel them with a potato peeler. Using a mandoline, slice beets about 1/8 of an inch thick. As you are slicing them, place them in a bowl with olive oil, vinegar, crushed garlic, thyme, and salt to marinate. Peel and slice all the beets. It is important to marinate them while still warm.

3. Preheat the oven to 380°F. Take the dough out of the fridge and roll it out. Because of the olive oil, it may not be holding firm, so I prefer making the beet crostata in a baking dish. Use an 8 inch round pan or a 6 x 9 inch rectangular one. Roll the dough so that there is a one-inch dough overhang when you place it in the baking dish.

4. Take the beets out of the marinade and layer half of them on the dough. Place the feta cheese in a food processor bowl, add a tablespoon of the marinade (olive oil, vinegar, garlic) and pulse. Add a second tablespoon of the marinade if your feta mixture is too thick. With a

spoon, distribute half of the feta cheese on the beets. Add the second layer of beets, and then place the rest of the feta cheese. If you are using walnuts, add them now. Flip the overhanging dough over the beets.

5. Bake for 50 minutes or until thoroughly cooked and golden brown. During the last 10 minutes, place a piece of parchment paper on the crostata to prevent the top dough from burning, while the bottom still needs to bake a little more. Sprinkle with fresh pepper before you serve.

Winter

Chocolate

Chocolate is a beloved ingredient that needs to be handled with care. To begin with, we need to temper the chocolate when the recipe calls for it. The good news is that we can melt the chocolate again if we fail the first time and temper it all over again. However, if we burn the chocolate, either by using the microwave to melt it or by leaving it in the bain-marie over boiling water for too long, the chocolate is destroyed and cannot be used anymore. Read the instructions on page 7 to see how to temper the chocolate.

If you are making chocolate candy of any type you may dip the filling in melted chocolate or use little silicon containers to create small chocolate candy (Chocolate with Mandarin recipe, page 16). To use silicone trays, you have to follow these steps.

1. Temper the chocolate.

2. Add the chocolate to a piping bag and distribute it to the sockets of the silicon tray.

3. Move the tray around so that the chocolate covers the walls of the little socket all around.

4. Turn the mold upside down over the bowl with the chocolate, and tap a few times to get rid of the excess chocolate. With a spatula, scrape the flat top of the tray.

5. Fill up the molds with the filling of your choice.

6. Pipe more chocolate in every little socket to seal the filling in and create a flat base for your chocolate candy.

7. Tap the silicone mold on the counter a few times to ensure that no air bubbles are trapped.

8. With a spatula, scrape the flat surface of the silicon mold again to even the surface.

9. Let the chocolates set and cool completely and then unmold.

Chocolate with Pepper or Salt (25) 🗒 🌾

250 grams or 9 ounces dark chocolate
2 grams of Cayenne pepper OR 3 grams of sea salt

1. Start by melting good quality dark chocolate over Bain Marie.

2. Temper the chocolate according to the instructions on page 7 but do not reheat the chocolate which is the second step of tempering. When it reaches 80-82℉ take it out and use it. For this recipe, we need the chocolate to be cooler than usual.

3. Fill a piping bag and use it to create small, round chocolate candy. Dust with pepper or sea salt, or divide the chocolate in two and use pepper on half of the chocolate and salt on the other half. I love green pepper. Experiment with various types of pepper to find your favorite.

Chocolate Truffle (24) 🌾

The king of all chocolate candy! Melts in your mouth, while bitter, sweet, buttery, and salty waves hit your taste buds, leaving you longing for the next one...

240 grams or 9 ounces dark chocolate, the highest quality
120 grams or 1/2 cup cream
30 grams or 2 tablespoons butter

120 grams or 4 ounces chocolate
120 grams or 1 1/2 cup unsweetened cocoa
3 grams or 1/4 teaspoon of sea salt

1. Chop the chocolate into small pieces and place them in a bowl.
2. In a small pot warm up the cream until it steams but does not come to a boil.
3. Pour the cream over the chocolate in the bowl and let it sit for three minutes, for the chocolate to soften. Stir the cream and the chocolate with a spatula until all the chocolate melts.
4. Add the butter, cut into cubes, and continue stirring until the sauce (it is called ganache) is completely smooth. Cover it up and let it cool for one hour in the refrigerator.
5. Place the ganache in a piping bag and form small balls, truffles, about the size of a walnut. Cover the truffles up with plastic wrap and let them cool down in the fridge for at least one hour. You may leave them in the fridge overnight.
6. In a container (glass or plastic) sift in the cocoa and with your fingers crush in the sea salt. Mix well. Now we have three options:
A. Place the truffles in the cocoa, swirl them around to cover them completely with the cocoa and... eat them.
B. Dip each one in 120 grams or 4 ounces melted and tempered chocolate and with a fork remove it, tap it 2-3 times, and let it cool on a platter covered with parchment paper. Place them in cocoa, swirl them around and they are ready. This is a good and easy option but creates a thick exterior chocolate covering. I much prefer option C.
C. Cover them with a very fine exterior chocolate layer by doing the following: Melt 120 grams or 4 ounces of chocolate and temper it. Now place one tablespoon of chocolate in your left palm (if you are right-handed). Place a truffle in your palm and with your fingers turn it around until it is completely covered. Place it in the cocoa container. Keep your right hand clean, so that you can add the chocolate to your left palm with it (always try to keep one hand clean in the kitchen). When you have enough truffles in the cocoa, swirl the box around until all are covered, and with your clean hand transfer them to a platter. Continue with the rest of the truffles until all are covered. You will not be sorry about how messy your hand and your kitchen become.

Make these when your niece and nephew visit you. You will make some great truffles together along with some precious memories of messy chocolate creation. Make sure you are not the one who gets to clean the kitchen, but you are the one who gets to eat the truffles.

Ann: *A flood of velvety chocolate in my mouth...*

Tahini and Honey Chocolate (24) 🗌 🌾

Tahini is sesame seed paste and is one of the healthiest ingredients you can eat. It has a slightly astringent kick and, when mixed with honey, it becomes incredibly tasty.

In case you do not have a silicone tray, you may use small paper cups to create individual chocolate candy.

250 grams or 9 ounces dark chocolate

<u>Filling</u>

3 tablespoons Tahini sauce

1 1/2 tablespoons honey

1/8 teaspoon salt

1 teaspoon cinnamon

1 tablespoon cognac (if you are not serving children)

1. Melt the chocolate and temper it.

2. With a piping bag, distribute half of the chocolate in silicone molds or paper cups. Place in the fridge for 5 minutes to let the chocolate set.

3. Mix the Tahini, honey, salt, cinnamon and cognac briefly, just until incorporated. With another piping bag place a small amount of this mixture in each mold.

4. Pipe the rest of the chocolate in the molds. Tap the tray a few times to release any trapped air, scrap the top of the mold with a spatula, and let the chocolates cool down and set.

Peanut butter chocolate candy (50) 🗌

This homemade candy, inspired by a well-known brand of peanut butter chocolate, is a big hit with our students. You have three options for forming them: 1) You can form the filling into small balls and dip them in chocolate. 2) You can spread half your chocolate in a 9x11 inch pan lined with parchment paper. Let it set in the fridge for a few minutes, spread the filling on top, and then end with the rest of the chocolate. 3) The most appealing and most time-consuming; spread a teaspoon of chocolate in small paper cups and let it set. Add a teaspoon of the filling and end with a teaspoon of chocolate.

500 grams or 18 oz chocolate + 1 tablespoon smooth peanut butter + 1/8 teaspoon salt

6 tablespoons powdered sugar

10 digestive cookies or graham cookies

1 jar smooth peanut butter (350 grams or 12 ounces)

1/4 teaspoon salt

1. In a bain-marie, melt the chocolate.
Add a tablespoon of peanut butter and 1/8 ts of salt.

2. In a food processor add the rest of the ingredients (use half the salt in this stage) and blend until well incorporated. Taste for salt. Some peanut butter brands are saltier than others. Decide if you will use all the salt or not, but in any case, the filling needs to be almost salty.

3. Form into small balls and dip them in chocolate or follow one of the options given above.

Grace: the bitter dark chocolate and sweet tahini inside paired so well together.
The perfect treat for after dinner.

Glazed Orange with Chocolate (36) 🍊 🌾

Orange with chocolate is one of my favorite combinations. These orange slices are superb. You may store them in an airtight container for months, either plain, half dipped in chocolate, or fully covered in it.

6 oranges
1200 grams or 6 cups water
600 grams or 3 cups sugar
100 grams or 1/3 cup corn syrup
A generous pinch of salt
250 grams or 8 oz dark chocolate
A pinch of salt

1. Wash the oranges with warm water to remove any protective wax from the peels. With a very sharp paring knife, slice them as consistently as possible. We are aiming at slightly less than 1/8 of an inch thickness but not as thin as 1/16 because the orange will tear up if the slices are this thin.

2. In a wide pot, place the water, sugar, and corn syrup. Stir the syrup to dissolve the sugar as much as possible. Turn the heat on at high. Once the syrup starts to boil, add salt and the orange slices carefully. Turn the heat to the lowest degree possible. Let the oranges boil in the syrup for 1 hour. Carefully shake the pot every now and then. Towards the end of the cooking time, check the water level often. If the heat is low enough you should have plenty of water to last one hour.

3. Remove the oranges from the syrup and arrange them on a wire rack to drain.

4. You have two options: either let the oranges dry for one or two days (depending on the heat and humidity of your house) or place them in the oven for one hour at 160°F to dry them. We need them to be dry enough that when you touch them your finger does not become sticky.

5. After the orange slices are dried and cool, melt the chocolate in a Bain Marie or the microwave. Temper the chocolate according to instructions on page 7. Add a pinch of salt. Dip the oranges in the melted chocolate, halfway through or completely, and place them on parchment paper to set.

Andrew: *Orange-you glad you can now make these?*

Halva

Halva is a whole category of desserts, and you might be surprised by how many different (very different) desserts are called Halva. What makes a dessert Halva is that it is made with 1 cup of ingredient A, 2 cups of ingredient B, 3 cups of C, and so on. They are very common in all Eastern cultures and the variety is endless. I am giving you only a few examples, my three favorite ones.

Halva with Semolina (8-12) 🗒

This is a dense cake with a sandy-like texture and a strong cinnamon flavor. Students call this "sand cake" because of its texture. It has very loyal friends or bitter enemies. There are no lukewarm feelings about this one. We serve it hot with vanilla or cinnamon ice cream. What is not to love?

1 cup vegetable oil (minus 1 tablespoon, because Halva gets too oily)
2 cups fine semolina or regular Cream of Wheat (not instant)
2 1/2 cups sugar (original recipe asks for 3 cups sugar)
4 cups water
1 tablespoon cinnamon + almonds or pistachios for decoration

Optional: Add half a cup of almonds, roughly chopped, in the semolina and oil mixture when it starts to become golden, 3-4 minutes after you start cooking it.

1. In a heavy saucepan add the oil and semolina and turn the heat to medium. Start stirring the mixture with a wooden spoon. In 3-4 minutes it will start to darken. If you are adding almonds, add them now. Cook a little longer, until there are browned crumbs of the semolina. Add the cinnamon and cook for one more minute. Take the saucepan off the heat.
2. Meanwhile, in a big pot, add 4 cups water and 2 1/2 cups sugar and bring to a boil. Once it starts to boil, briefly pull the pan off the heat and very carefully add the semolina mixture. Mix well and return to the heat. It will splash the lava hot mixture so you have to be prepared. Get the biggest lid you have and use it as a shield. Also, wear a glove. Mix it until it thickens up and the spatula leaves a trail on the bottom of the pot, which is going to be in one or two minutes. Take it off the heat and transfer it into a bundt cake form or in small individual forms for a fancier presentation.
3. Let it set for ten minutes and then unmold it by shaking the form with a big plate under it while you are wearing mittens. Sprinkle with some nuts (if you want), more cinnamon, and serve with vanilla or -better- cinnamon ice cream. As I said, it has very loyal friends.
This is considered one of the easiest and probably the quickest dessert to make. You need about 5 minutes to cook the semolina with the oil and another 2 in the boiling water and you have a dessert ready to be enjoyed with ice cream.

Emily: *I think about your cinnamon sand cake at least once a week*
(Emily was in Greece in the Spring of 2018).

Tahini and honey Halva ⬚ ⬚

This Halva is one of the healthiest preparations you can put in your mouth. It is also the simplest. All you need to do is find Tahini sauce, either in delicatessen stores, ethnic food groceries, or online. Mix 1 part honey with 2 parts tahini. Mix well and it will instantly thicken up to a velvety sauce, packed with vitamins, antioxidants, and anti-inflammatories. Sprinkle some cinnamon on top and eat on bread or with apples or with good yellow cheese, like gruyere. (Do not add cinnamon if you are eating it with cheese.)

Brooklyn: *Tahini and honey with either a banana or a sliced up apple was my favorite snack in between classes*

Halva with carrot from India (24) ⬚ ⬚

1 cup (minus 2 tablespoons) of vegetable oil or melted cleared butter (page 6).
2 cups cornstarch or cornflour
2 cups sugar (the original recipe asks for 3 cups)
4 cups water
5 packed cups of carrots, peeled and grated
For flavoring use, 2 teaspoons of flower water or rose water (I think rose water has a heavy aroma, whereas flower water has a delicate, Jasmine aroma). You will find both in Middle Eastern Markets, delicatessen stores, or big supermarkets. If you do not like any of these flavorings, try **2 tablespoons of freshly squeezed orange juice.**
Topping: Two tablespoons of ground pistachio.

1. Wash and peel the carrots and grate them either by hand or in the food processor. Add the water, sugar, and carrots to a heavy pot and bring to a boil. Lower the heat and simmer for 25-30 minutes, stirring often, until most of the water is absorbed. When there is little water left in the pot, add the flower water or the cinnamon and ground cloves.

2. Meanwhile, in a heavy saucepan add the oil or butter (your preference) and the cornstarch and stir very well to incorporate before you start cooking it. If you are using butter melt it first. It will become a thick paste. Cook over low heat for 4-5 minutes and set aside.

3. When the carrot mixture comes back to a boil after it has been flavored, add the cooked cornstarch mixture to the carrot mixture and continue cooking, while stirring constantly, until the mixture thickens up and becomes slightly translucent. There should be no white cornstarch visible anymore.

4. Transfer to a serving dish or an ungreased bundt form. Let it cool completely before you unmold the bundt form. Sprinkle with grated pistachio. I love it when it is cold out of the fridge, but you can also consume it at room temperature.

This is a rich dessert, so consider making half the recipe if you are serving a few people.

Chocolate Souffle (8)

75 grams or 5 tablespoons butter
80 grams or 10 tablespoons flour
700 grams or 3 cups milk
120 grams or 4 ounces dark chocolate
1/8 teaspoon salt
1 teaspoon vanilla extract
100 grams or 1/2 cup sugar
3 eggs + 2 egg whites (two additional egg whites are optional)
A pinch of salt
A tablespoon of sugar

Ice cream or heavy cream to serve.

1. Turn the oven to 380°F.
2. In a pot melt the butter over medium heat. Add the flour and stir until there is no visible trace of flour anymore.
3. Add the milk, a cup at a time, stirring constantly until your mixture turns into a thick cream. It might take 3 cups or even 3 1/2 cups. Taste the cream. If you can still taste the flour, add half a cup more milk and keep cooking while stirring for a couple more minutes.
4. Take off the heat and add the chocolate, cut in pieces, salt and vanilla. Let it sit for a few minutes until all the chocolate is melted. Add the sugar and stir. You may add less sugar (as little as two tablespoons) or more (as much as one cup) depending on how sweet or bitter you like your chocolate. A half-cup is what I normally use.
5. Add the egg yolks to the chocolate mixture and stir.
6. In a mixer bowl, add the egg whites and start whisking. Three egg whites are the minimum, and you may add two more (five in total) so that the final souffle will be very light and airy. Add a pinch of salt and a tablespoon of sugar to create a stable meringue. Once the meringue is thick enough for the whisk to leave a trail, turn the mixer off and fold the meringue into the chocolate mixture. Fold with a spatula, or even better, a whisk with big strokes going from top to bottom while at the same time you turn the bowl with your other hand in the opposite direction.
7. Butter a souffle dish (high straight sides). Add a tablespoon of flour or sugar to coat the dish, and transfer the chocolate into the mold. Place it in the oven and bake for 50-55 minutes until the souffle has formed a nice crust on top but is still a little wiggly. Alternatively, you may use 8 ramekins. In this case, you will need to bake them only for 30-35 minutes.
8. Serve immediately with ice cream or lightly whipped heavy cream.

Brooke Elizabeth: *Natasa's chocolate soufflé... I dream about that stuff!!*

Italian Lemon and Ricotta Cake (8) 🌾

This is very tasty, light, tangy and rich all at the same time. My mom, who is not a dessert person, loves how lemony and light this cake is.

120 grams or 1 stick unsalted butter (room temperature)
150 grams or 3/4 cup sugar
250 grams or 1 cup ricotta cheese
1/2 teaspoon vanilla extract
A pinch of salt
3 egg yolks
Zest of one lemon
2 or 3 tablespoons lemon juice (depending on the acidity of the juice)
150 grams or 1 1/2 cups almond powder
1 teaspoon baking powder
3 egg whites
50 grams or 1/4 cup sugar
Powdered sugar and almond flakes for decoration

1. Preheat the oven to 350°F. Line the bottom of a springform pan with parchment paper and butter it. Alternatively, you may butter a nice baking dish or ramekins and use them so that you will not have to unmold the cake, which might be tricky since it is such a light and delicate cake. (Gluten free cakes are always delicate).
2. In a mixer bowl, add the butter and sugar and whisk at medium speed until the mixture becomes lighter in color and doubles its volume, about 5-7 minutes. Add the ricotta, vanilla, salt, egg yolks, lemon juice and zest, and continue whisking until all are incorporated. Turn the mixer off and fold in the almond powder and the baking powder. (Use 2 tablespoons of lemon juice, try a little batter, and decide if you want a stronger lemony flavor by adding another tablespoon of juice. Acidity in lemon juice varies depending on the lemons).
3. In another bowl whisk the egg whites at medium speed and, when they start to foam, add, gradually, 1/4 cup sugar. Turn the mixer to medium-high and continue whisking until the whisk leaves a trail on the meringue and when you lift the whisk, soft peaks form. Fold the meringue into the mixture, transfer it to the pan, and level the top. If you are using ramekins, divide the mixture into eight small ones or six medium ones.
4. Bake for 45 minutes (25-30 if you are using ramekins) or until the mixture takes on a nice golden color. Let it cool. Transfer to a platter and sprinkle the top with almond flakes and powdered sugar.
I like to serve this cake with good lemon tea.

Tip: When you grate lemon zest or orange zest, do it directly over the dessert. Most of the flavor is in the oil that splatters while you are grating. If you grate the zest over a plate and then transfer it to the desert, most of the aromatic oil is wasted.

Grace: *Light, sweet and so perfectly soft! The light lemony flavor paired so well with the almonds*

Austrian Sacher Torte (8)

This is a stunning dessert with a very rich history. You can find it in Vienna in every pastry shop. The taste, texture, and aroma of this cake are unparalleled. It is not difficult, you will just use a lot of bowls. Believe me, you will not regret making it.

5 egg whites at room temperature
100 grams or 1/2 cup sugar

5 egg yolks
60 grams or 1/2 cup powdered sugar
130 grams or 9 tablespoons butter (very soft)

130 grams or 1 cup flour
130 grams or 4 1/2 ounces melted chocolate
1/4 teaspoon sea salt
1 teaspoon vanilla extract
200 grams or 3/4 cup strawberry marmalade
<u>**Frosting**</u>
200 grams or 1 cup sugar
90 grams or 6 tablespoons water
100 grams or 3 1/2 ounces chocolate

1. In a mixer bowl, add 5 egg whites and one half cup sugar and whisk until a stiff meringue is formed (when you turn the bowl upside down the meringue is not falling out).
2. Preheat the oven to 360°F. Butter a 9 or 10 inch round pan with a removable bottom or place parchment paper on the bottom of a regular pan. Melt 4 1/2 ounces chocolate.
3. In another bowl whisk 5 egg yolks with the powdered sugar and the butter until completely incorporated. Slowly and lightly fold in the flour and the melted chocolate with the sea salt and vanilla extract. Do not overwork the mixture (no need to be fully incorporated) because it will thicken up too much. Fold the meringue in with soft and steady movements (now the mixture needs to be fully incorporated). Transfer to the buttered pan and bake for 55-60 minutes or until a knife comes out clean when you insert it in the middle of the cake.
4. Take the cake out of the oven and let it cool slightly. With a bread knife, you can cut the top, puffed dome off so that the cake is flat. Unmold it by flipping it upside down on a platter. While the cake is still hot, brush the marmalade on the flat surface of the cake and let it cool completely. Move the cake to a wire rack.
5. In a pot add the frosting ingredients and bring to a boil over medium heat, stirring constantly. We want the mixture to reach 225°F if you have a thermometer, or mark four minutes after it has started boiling. Take the pot off the heat. Place it over a bowl with cold water and start stirring the chocolate with a spatula to cool it down (tempering the chocolate). When the frosting starts to thicken and your spatula leaves a trail (about 140°F), bring the pot over the heat again for 10 seconds (chocolate should be 170°F) and then pour immediately over the cake. The wire rack is important because the chocolate will drip. The chocolate will harden to a crunchy, shiny, tasty frosting. You are most welcome…

Luke: *I think about the Vienna dessert every day!*

Tip: *This dessert traditionally is served with chantilly (whipped cream). I made small chocolate bowls by dipping round ice cubes in melted chocolate, see page 7. I let the ice melt, and the chocolate dry and then I filled the small chocolate bowls with unsweetened whipped heavy cream. You could also dip small balloons in melted chocolate to create small chocolate bowls.*

French Mont Blanc *(8)*

This dessert is named after the highest mountain in the Alps and comes in many variations: in a pie shell or on a cookie, with pastry cream or whipped cream, with or without meringue: but the form always has to be a mountain-like buildup of chestnut puree. When we lived in France, I do not think I ever ordered a dessert during winter that was not the Mont Blanc.

Tart Dough
50 grams or 1/4 cup sugar
60 grams or 4 tablespoons butter (room temperature)
130 grams or 1 cup flour
1 teaspoon baking powder
1 egg yolk
Filling
400 grams or 14 ounces chestnuts (in a vacuum package)
120 grams or 1/2 cup milk
120 grams or 1 cup powdered sugar
3 tablespoons rum
Meringue puffs
2 egg whites
100 grams or 1/2 cup sugar
1 teaspoon cornstarch
1 teaspoon white vinegar
Topping
1 cup heavy cream
1 tablespoon powdered sugar

1. In a food processor, add the sugar and butter and pulse. Add the flour and baking powder and pulse until well incorporated. Finally, add the egg yolk and work just until all ingredients are incorporated. Wrap the dough in plastic wrap and let it rest in the fridge for twenty minutes. Roll out between two parchment papers, cut in discs, and place in individual tartlets that you have buttered. Prick the dough with a fork. Alternatively, cut the rolled dough into 3-inch diameter flat discs, like cookies. Bake at 350°F until fully baked for 15-20 minutes.

2. Make the meringue puffs. Make sure they fit on the tartelettes, so they need to be around 1.5 το 2 inches in diameter for a 3-inch cookie. Please read the meringue-making instructions on page 52. Since these are small, you will need about one hour of baking.

3. You can either choose vacuum-packed or canned chestnuts. The problem with canned chestnuts is that they have added sugar or salt and the texture is inconsistent between brands. I prefer to use French vacuum-packaged chestnuts. Place the chestnuts in the food processor and work them. Slowly add the milk and the sugar. You should end up with a very creamy texture and thin consistency. Transfer the mixture to a pot, add the rum, and cook over low heat, stirring constantly with a spatula until the mixture thickens up and resembles the consistency of mashed potato. It will take two to four minutes. Let the mixture cool completely. Transfer the chestnut mixture to a piping bag that is fitted with a round star tip, or (if you use Wilton) a triple star or a leaf tip nozzle.

4. Beat the heavy cream with the powdered sugar until thick peaks form. With another piping bag, place a drop of the cream on a tartlet or cookie and then add a meringue puff. With the Chestnut piping bag, start forming concentric, stacking, decreasing diameter circles, starting from the bottom and working your way to the top. Finish with a drop of whipped cream or dust the Chestnut "mountain" with some powdered sugar.

I made and photographed these on a snowy day in Athens, where it snows every 4 or 5 years...

French Poire: Belle Hélène (6) 🗒 🌾

Poached pears are such a lovely and elegant dessert. They are quite easy to make and let's not forget that they are healthy! There are two versions of poached pears; one is poached in red wine and the other, which I give here, is poached in syrup and using a nice sauce on top. I use strawberry sauce, or you can make a chocolate ganache (see page 83).

6 pears. They have to be firm but ripe. Williams or Comice work best.
150 grams or 3/4 cup sugar
2 sticks cinnamon
4 cloves
1-star anise

1. In a pot add six cups of water, sugar, and spices and let it come to a boil. Turn the heat off and let the flavors infuse while you are preparing the pears.
2. Trim the bottom of the pear so that it can stand straight. Do not remove the stem, it looks lovely, and do not core the pears. In my opinion, the seeds offer a good taste to the pears, and also they have a lot of piktine, which is transferred to the syrup. Use a peeler to peel them carefully. Place them in the pot with the syrup. The syrup should cover them completely. Add some water if you need to. Take a piece of parchment paper and create a cheminee (see below) and cover them with the parchment paper directly on the surface of the water. Boil for 25 to 30 minutes until the pears are soft when inserting a knife. Let them cool in the syrup. You can store them in the fridge for several days in their own syrup until you consume them.
3. When you are ready to serve, take them out of the syrup and add five or six strawberries (fresh or frozen) to the syrup, or two tablespoons of strawberry jam. Let the syrup boil for ten minutes and serve next to the pears after you pass it through a sieve to ensure a completely smooth and transparent sauce.

They are great with ice cream, too.

Cheminée. This is a French word that simply means chimney. Take a piece of parchment paper big enough to cover the top of your pot. Fold it in half, and then fold again twice, each time down the middle, to create a triangle. Place the folded paper above the pot, positioning the center of the paper/corner of the triangle above the center of the pot, and trace with a pencil the edge of your pot, in order to measure its radius. Cut off a small part of the corner of the triangle and also cut around the perimeter (across the line you traced in the previous step) to create a disc  with a hole in the middle. This is very handy when cooking and boiling vegetables. It prevents the boiling water from evaporating quickly and helps keep the whole vegetable underwater.

Alex: *Can we have this every day? Pearleeees?*

Old Italian Potato Cake (8-10) 🌾

Interesting, different, delicious, and gluten-free! A very pleasant cake that reminds me of a dense cheesecake that will surprise you very pleasantly! Comes from an old Italian cookbook from the Tuscan region.

1 pound or 2 medium potatoes
120 grams or 1 stick butter (room temperature)
100 grams or 1/2 cup sugar
4 egg yolks
1 teaspoon lemon zest (you will need two lemons or one lemon and one orange)
1/8 teaspoon nutmeg (preferably freshly grated)
1 teaspoon vanilla extract
30 grams or 1/4 cup almond flour (you can substitute with wheat flour if allergic to nuts)
4 egg whites
50 grams or 1/4 cup sugar
A pinch of salt
1/2 cup pine nuts or almond flakes (optional but highly recommended)
powdered sugar for dusting

1. Wash the potatoes thoroughly and place them in plenty of water in a pot with a teaspoon of salt. Bring to a soft boil and let the potatoes cook until very soft. Remove from the water and let them cool slightly. As soon as you can handle them, peel them and mash them in a food mill. If you do not have one, mash them by hand and pass them through a sieve so that there are no lumps (the cake will be very unpleasant if there are). Do not use an electric whisk as it will break the starch too far and turn the mashed potatoes into an elastic mixture. Let the mashed potatoes cool completely, uncovered so that they lose as much moisture as possible.
2. Turn the oven to 400°F. Butter a 9 inch round springform and line it with parchment paper.
3. In the mixer bowl place the butter and 1/2 cup sugar and whisk at medium speed until the mixture starts to lighten in color, about 5-7 minutes. Add the yolks, lemon zest, nutmeg (fresh nutmeg brings a wonderful, delicate flavor), and vanilla, and continue whisking until all are incorporated.
4. Turn the mixer on low speed and add the potatoes alternating with the almond flour. Mix until incorporated.
5. In a clean mixer bowl add the 4 egg whites and start whisking at medium speed. Once the eggs start to froth, add a pinch of salt and 1/4 cup sugar. Whisk until they turn into a stiff meringue. It is very important for the meringue to be well beaten to give us volume later.
6. Fold 1/3 of the meringue into the cake batter to loosen it and then add the rest of the meringue and fold. Transfer the batter to the form, level the top, and sprinkle with the pine nuts or almond flakes. If there is a nut allergy, you can skip the nuts, but otherwise don't, because they add a welcoming texture. Bake for 45-50 minutes until the cake takes a wonderful golden brown color. When the cake is completely cool, dust it with powdered sugar.

Portuguese Pastel de Nata (24)

Pastel de Nata is a world-famous dessert that was created by Portuguese monks in the 18th century. It has a delicious lemony custard on a crunchy base. Because the base dough is quite complicated to make, I tested a few alternative options and came up with this version that is not far from the original in flavor and texture but it is a lot easier to make. The recipe for the cream is very close to the original.

To make this dessert you will need individual pie shells or tartelettes. A silicone mold for macarons will also do. The sides should be around 1 inch high and the base 2-3 inches.

1 package of phyllo dough
120 grams or 1 stick butter, melted
120 grams or 1 cup powdered sugar
<u>Filling</u>
350 grams or 1 1/2 cups milk
25 grams or 3 tablespoons flour
265 grams or 1 1/3 cup sugar
100 grams or 1/2 cup water
1 Stick cinnamon
2 strips lemon peel
6 egg yolks
1 teaspoon pure vanilla extract or 1 vanilla bean

1. Make the filling first. Place the cold milk and the flour in a pot and stir until the flour is dissolved. If you are using a vanilla bean, cut it in half, scrape the seeds and add it now. Turn the heat on, stirring constantly, until the mixture thickens up slightly (honey consistency).

2. In another pot add the sugar, water, cinnamon stick, and lemon peel. Bring to a boil over medium-high heat and let the temperature rise to 220°F (if you have a thermometer) or about five minutes after it starts to boil. Take off the heat and in a thin thread add this syrup to the milk mixture stirring constantly. Let it cool slightly and add the egg yolks and vanilla extract (if you are not using the vanilla bean) and stir thoroughly. The mixture will be thin. Pass through a sieve into a jar, for ease later, and cover with plastic wrap. Put the egg whites in the fridge, cover them, and use them to make another dessert like Pistachio cake or Panna cotta.

3. Preheat the oven to 475°F. Take one phyllo sheet out of the package and place it flat in front of you. Brush with the butter so that there is a very thin layer of butter on the whole surface of the phyllo. Take a tablespoon of the powdered sugar and through a strainer dust the whole phyllo. Place the second phyllo exactly on top of the first one. Butter it and dust once more with a tablespoon of powdered sugar. Repeat the process with the third phyllo and finish with a fourth one. Do not butter this one. This method creates a very tasty buttery crust.

4, Choose a mold or tartelette and look for a round cookie cutter that will cut a base that covers the bottoms and sides of the mold. For example, the base of my mold is 2 ¼ inches and the height is 1 inch, so I choose a cookie cutter that is 2 1/4 +1+1 (for both sides) equals 4 1/4 inches in diameter. Cut the layered phyllo with the cookie cutter and place the phyllo in the molds that you have buttered first. Press the dough to fit well in the mold.

5. Divide the cream into the molds and bake in the hot oven for 10 to 15 minutes, depending on the size, until very well baked and dark spots appear on your pastry. Take them out of the oven, let them cool slightly, and unmold. Dust with powdered sugar and serve.

Morgan: *This is not from Portugal! It's from HEAVEN!*

Lemon Cake (10)

4 eggs
200 grams or 1 cup sugar
100 grams or 1/2 cup yogurt
120 grams or 1 stick butter, melted and cooled
Zest of one lemon
80 grams or 7 tablespoons lemon juice
30 grams or 2 tablespoons dark rum or cognac
200 grams or 1 1/2 cup flour
2 teaspoon baking powder
A pinch of salt
Icing 1: Cream cheese frosting
250 grams or 1 cup cream cheese
125 grams or 1 cup powdered sugar (you might need 1 1/2 cups)
A pinch of salt
Lemon zest from half lemon
Icing 2: Swiss Meringue
3 egg whites
130 grams or 2/3 cup sugar
Lemon zest from half lemon

1. Preheat the oven to 350°F. In a mixer bowl place the eggs with the sugar and beat at medium speed until they turn pale yellow, 7-8 minutes. Lower the speed to slow and add the yogurt, melted butter, lemon juice, lemon zest, and rum or cognac and mix until incorporated.

2. Turn the mixer off and sift in the flour, together with the baking powder and salt, all the while folding it slowly into the egg mixture. When the flour mixture is all incorporated, transfer to an 8 or 9-inch buttered cake bundt pan or loaf pan (11 or 12 inches long) and bake for 55-60 minutes or until a knife comes out clean when inserted in the middle of the cake, and a deep golden color is achieved.

3. Take the cake out of the oven and let it cool down. Ten or fifteen minutes later unmold it on a platter. You have three options: A) Serve the cake with ice cream.

B) Serve with cream cheese frosting: whip one cup of cream cheese with one cup of powdered sugar, a pinch of salt, and a little lemon zest until a thick frosting has formed.

C) Serve with Swiss Meringue frosting (picture): Add 3 egg whites and 2/3 cup sugar in a heat-proof bowl and place over a pot with simmering water in a Bain Marie. Whisk with a handheld mixer until the mixture reaches 150°F, about 5 minutes. You will see that it thickens up noticeably, resembling a marshmallow spread and feels warm if you touch it. Take the meringue off the heat and transfer it to a stand mixer bowl. Whisk at low speed for 10 minutes until it cools down noticeably. Transfer to a piping bag and create a nice pattern on your cake. You can dust with lemon zest or, alternatively, burn the top of the Swiss Meringue with a torch (see page 75), for a lovely broiled s'mores taste on the cake.

Elizabeth: This was absolutely divine, and I'd give anything for another piece right now!

German Cheesecake: Käsekuchen (12)

The texture of this pie is unbelievably airy and light, and the taste is supreme. We have substituted the German cheese, Quark, with Greek yogurt and the result is excellent.

Pie Crust

125 grams or 1/2 cup and 2 tablespoons sugar
120 grams or 1 stick butter
300 grams 2 1/4 cups flour
1/2 teaspoon baking powder
1 teaspoon vanilla extract
A pinch of salt
1 egg

Filling

240 grams or 1 cup milk
45 grams or 7 tablespoons cornstarch (be very precise here, leveling the spoon)
85 grams or ½ cup vegetable oil
150 grams or 3/4 cup sugar
1/2 teaspoon vanilla extract
3 egg yolks
200 grams or 1 cup yogurt 2% or 5% fat content
3 egg whites
A pinch of salt
Optional for decoration: A can of sour cherries (7 ounces) + 1 tablespoon cornstarch + 1 tablespoon sugar OR fresh cherries OR fruit of your choice

1. Preheat the oven to 370°F.
2. In a food processor, add the sugar and butter and incorporate. Add the flour, baking powder, salt, and vanilla and mix. Add the egg and pulse the food processor briefly, until the dough starts to hold together. Place it between two parchment papers and roll into a flat disc, big enough to cover your pie dish base and sides. Wrap your dough with a plastic film, and place it in the fridge on a cookie sheet for twenty minutes. Transfer it to a buttered springform (9 or 10 inches in diameter) prick with a fork several times and bake for 15 minutes.
3. Filling: In a bowl mix the milk with the cornstarch until it is dissolved and add the rest of the ingredients except the egg whites. Mix with a handheld mixer until completely smooth.
4. In the mixer bowl add the egg whites and a pinch of salt and whisk until stiff peaks are formed. Fold the white egg mixture into the rest of the filling with smooth and gentle strokes until incorporated. Add this filling to the partially baked pie shell.
5. Bake for another 40 or 45 minutes until the pie is set, even if slightly bouncy.
6. You can serve it plain or you may add the canned cherries on top after you drain them. Save the juice from the can and put it in a small pot with a tablespoon of cornstarch and a tablespoon of sugar and cook, stirring constantly until it thickens up 3-4 minutes. Pour over the cherries.

If you make it in the summer use fresh cherries or use any fruit or berries you prefer.

Ann: *This filling reminds me of that fluffy Japanese cheesecake!!! So good!*

Orange souffle in Oranges (8)

Fancy, beautiful, tasty, and very impressive. You could simplify it by baking the souffle in ramekins — individual souffle holders — or even in one big souffle dish.

8 big nice oranges
75 grams or 5 tablespoons butter
80 grams or 10 tablespoons flour
240 grams or 1 cup milk 3.5%
1 teaspoon vanilla extract
1/2 teaspoon salt
125 grams or 1/2 cup + 2 tablespoons sugar
3 eggs yolks + 3 egg whites divided
Optional: A cup of fresh cranberries or blueberries for decoration.

1. Start by washing the oranges very well. Trim the bottom to create a flat base and cut the top off, creating a hole about 1 1/2 to 1 3/4 inches in diameter. We need to separate the orange peel from the flesh. With a sharp knife trace the hole into the orange, going as deep as you need to cut out the inside orange flesh but not damage the peel. With the help of a spoon remove most of the flesh that you just cut. Go around the orange from the inside a few times with the spoon to remove as much juice as possible. Do all the work on the inside of the orange over a bowl to collect the juice and the flesh. Take out two cups of orange juice and set them aside to use later. Set the empty orange shell in a pan. When the oranges are emptied and lined up in the pan, sprinkle a pinch of salt inside every orange.

2. Turn the oven on to 380°F.

3. In a pot over medium heat melt 5 tablespoons butter and then add 10 tablespoons flour, while stirring. When all the flour is incorporated, add one cup of milk and stir well. Take the two cups of orange juice we saved earlier and add them gradually to the butter mixture while it is cooking and thickening. Taste the cream. If you can still taste the flour add 1/2 cup more milk. You should have a tasty and thick cream.

4. Add the vanilla, a pinch of salt, 1/2 cup sugar (100 grams), and three egg yolks to the mixture. Zest the orange tops you cut off and add the zest to the mixture, or use the zest of another orange, not one of the eight you are already using.

5. In a clean bowl whisk the egg whites at medium speed. Add two tablespoons of sugar (25 grams) and bring the speed up to high. Whisk until stiff peaks are formed.

6. With soft movements fold the meringue into the batter. Transfer the batter into a piping bag for filling the oranges. This is the easiest, fastest, and cleanest way to fill the oranges. Fill the oranges up to a little lower than the rim. The filling will rise during baking. There will be some filling left, and you can fill three or four ramekins with it. (At this point, if you are not ready to bake and serve, you may cover the filled oranges and refrigerate for a few hours.)

7. Optional: Spread any fruit you like on the bottom of the pan, to use as support to keep the oranges in place while baking. I like to use berries (any kind I might have) and/or apple chunks. Drizzle 1/2 cup of orange juice on the fruit at the bottom of the pan. They will also be delicious.

8. Bake for 30 minutes or until the top is golden brown. Remove from the oven, sprinkle with powdered sugar and serve immediately.

Riley*: If you made angel soup, this is what it would taste like…*

Spicy Chocolate Tart (8-12) 🌾

Base: Dacquoise
3 egg whites
200 grams or 1 cup sugar
A pinch of salt
55 grams or 1/2 cup powdered almond
55 grams or 1/2 cup powdered hazelnuts

Filling Ganache
60 grams or 1/4 cup milk
1 tablespoon cinnamon + 1/2 teaspoon ground cloves + 1/4 teaspoon nutmeg + 1 anise
OR one teaspoon of white peppercorns OR spices of your choice
350 grams or 1 1/2 cup cream
350 dark or 12 ounces chocolate chopped
30 grams or 2 tablespoons butter
1/8 teaspoon sea salt
A tablespoon of cocoa

Mietek: I was only going to have a piece of it with my coffee.
Never intended to finish the whole dish...

1. Start by infusing the milk with the spices of your choice. In a small pot warm up 50 grams of milk with all the spices until it starts to boil. Take off the heat and cover it completely with plastic wrap to let the flavors infuse. You may try any other spice or combination of spices. Lately, I like to infuse the milk with a teaspoon of white peppercorns. The final taste of the ganache is exquisite.

2. Make the dacquoise, which is the base of your tart (pictured here). Preheat the oven to 225°F on the air setting. Prepare an 8 or 9 inch round form with a removable base, line it with parchment paper and butter it. A baking ring would work, also.

3. In the clean bowl of your mixer, add the egg whites and start whisking at medium speed. When foam starts to form, add the sugar gradually. When all the sugar is added, turn the speed on high. Add a pinch of salt and whisk until firm peaks are formed. Turn the mixer off and add the almond and hazelnut powders, gradually, folding with soft movements from top to bottom with your right hand while turning the bowl counterclockwise with your left.

4. Transfer the mixture to a piping bag with a big round tip and start piping into the paper-lined 8 or 9-inch springform or on parchment paper (if using a baking ring 8 or 9-inch diameter). Start from the outside in a spiral motion towards the center of the form, leaving no gaps between the rings. This meringue with nut powder is called Dacquoise.

5. Take the Dacquoise to the oven and bake for 90 minutes. Turn the oven off and let the Dacquoise cool completely in the oven.

6. In another pot warm the cream until it steams but does not boil. Pour over the chocolate that you have already chopped. Let it stand for two minutes and then incorporate by stirring with a spatula. When completely smooth, add the butter. Add the milk through a sieve to catch all of the spices. Mix again and let the chocolate sauce cool while the dacquoise is getting ready. This sauce is called Ganache.

7. When the dacquoise is completely cool and the ganache has started to set (consistency of thick honey), pour the chocolate over the dacquoise, sprinkle with a pinch of sea salt and the cocoa powder, let it set for a couple of hours and serve. You can use any kind of jam for decoration. You may also store it in the fridge for a few days, completely covered. You will fall in love with the rich velvet chocolate.

Tip: Both components of this dessert, the dacquoise and the ganache, are amongst the best components in classical pastry making, and I would encourage you to experiment and use them in other desserts as well. Dacquoise, for example, can substitute very well for any pre-baked tart base. Ganache can be used plain or with spices to accompany any dessert, including fruit or ice cream. You can also experiment with various spices, using the method described here, to give your ganache your favorite aroma and flavor.

My Mom's cheese pies (24)

These are excellent cheese pies, and you can use your favorite cheese or experiment with different cheeses to achieve different results. The dough is crunchy and deeply tasty!

Dough
200 grams or 7 ounces (1 container) Greek yogurt 2%
110 grams or 1/2 cup olive oil
200 grams or 1 1/2 cups flour
1 tablespoon baking powder
A pinch of salt
90 grams or 3 ounces freshly grated gruyere or Pecorino or the cheese of your choice
Filling
200 grams or 7 ounces feta cheese
50 grams or 2 ounces ricotta cheese or cream cheese
1 egg
Fresh pepper
Fresh nutmeg (optional)
1 egg yolk
You will need more flour or cornstarch for dusting.

1. In a bowl place the yogurt and olive oil and mix with a wooden spoon. Start adding the flour, baking powder, and a pinch of salt. When the mixture thickens up, start kneading with your hand, lightly, adding just enough flour until the dough is not sticking to your hands anymore. Do not add more flour. Add the grated cheese and knead until just incorporated. Cover with a kitchen towel and set aside. It needs to rest for at least 30 minutes.
2. Turn the oven to 380°F.
3. In a food processor add the feta, ricotta, or cream cheese and the egg and blend until the mixture is smooth. Grate fresh pepper and nutmeg. Mix a bit longer, to incorporate the spices in the filling.
4. Divide the dough into small balls and roll them to a thickness of 1/4 of an inch. Dust with flour to facilitate the rolling or, preferably, dust with cornstarch for a crunchier cheese pie. Cut the rolled dough with a round cookie cutter into discs. Dip your finger in a glass of water and run it around the perimeter of the disc, so that the dough will seal well. Add a teaspoon of the filling in the middle of each disc, fold the dough in half over the filling and press the edges well with a fork to seal. You may also use your fingers to create a beautiful pattern as you seal the two sides of the dough. Arrange on a cookie sheet and brush the top with beaten egg yolk. Bake in the oven for 30 minutes and serve. You can save them in an airtight container for 2 or 3 days at room temperature or in the fridge for a couple of weeks.

Christmas

Christmas Cookies: Kourampies (48)

Around the Christmas period in Greece, every bakery, cafe, convenience store, gas station (you get the idea) offers two kinds of Christmas cookies: kourampies and melomakarona. They are both delectable. They both keep fresh and wonderful for weeks, thus making them ideal for the long Greek holiday season. This is the recipe for kourampies.

240 grams or 2 sticks unsalted butter, cold cut in small cubes
10 grams or 1 tablespoon sugar
60 grams or 1/2 cup powdered sugar
1 teaspoon vanilla extract
500 grams or 4 cups (minus 2 tablespoons) flour
1 teaspoon baking powder
30 grams or 2 tablespoons dark rum or cognac
30 grams or 2 tablespoons butter
120 grams or 1 cup roughly chopped almonds
A pinch of salt
<u>Topping</u>
Flour water (has a delicate jasmine aroma)
3 cups powdered sugar for dusting

1. Place the butter, two sugars, and vanilla in a mixer bowl and start whisking at medium speed until the mixture is very light and fluffy approximately 20 minutes. This extensive

whisking will give your cookies an extremely light texture that will make them irresistible.

2. In the meantime chop the almonds roughly (4-6 pieces per almond) and place them in a heavy saucepan along with two tablespoons of butter and a generous pinch of salt. Sauté the almonds for four or five minutes until they start to brown and the butter starts to burn. Once a wonderful nutty/buttery aroma fills the kitchen, turn the heat off immediately and set the almonds aside to let them cool completely.

3. Preheat the oven to 350°F. When the butter/sugar mixture is very light in color, almost white, turn the mixer down to the slowest speed and add the flour with the baking powder in three or four batches. You will need to scrape the walls of your mixer. Add the rum or cognac and the cooled browned almonds. Make sure you add all the almonds and the butter but not the brown burned particles which are at the bottom of the saucepan. As soon as the almonds are incorporated, turn the mixer off.

4. Shape your dough into small balls and place them on parchment paper on a cookie sheet. Bake for 20-25 minutes, depending on their size until the cookies start to turn golden.

5. Take out of the oven. If you have flower water, (not rose water, which is very strong) sprinkle a little (2 TB) on the cookies with your fingers. Flower water is very pleasant and has a delicate jasmine fragrance. You can find it in Middle Eastern markets and big supermarkets in the international section. Let the kourampies cool completely.

7. Roll the cookies in powdered sugar and place them on a platter. Dust with some more powdered sugar.

Christmas cookies: Melomakarona

This is a completely different cookie, but just as common and iconic for Greek Christmas.

Cookies

210 grams or 7 ounces olive oil or sunflower oil
130 grams or 1/2 cup + 2 tablespoons fresh orange juice
30 grams or 2 tablespoons cognac
20 grams or 1 tablespoon honey
80 grams or 6 tablespoons sugar
Zest of one orange
1 teaspoon baker's ammonia (you may substitute with baking powder)
1 tablespoon cinnamon
1/2 teaspoon ground cloves
460 grams or 3 1/2 cups flour
30 grams or 2 tablespoons semolina
100 grams or 1 cup walnut powder

Syrup

1 cup sugar
1 cup water
2-3 strips of orange peel
1 cup honey
Walnuts or pistachios for decoration

Let me start by saying that baker's ammonia was used as the primary leavening agent before baking powder. In fact, you may substitute baker's ammonia with baking powder, as baker's ammonia produces a wonderful, feathery, crunchier crumb. The downside is that while the cookies are baking, the baker's ammonia produces a strong unpleasant smell. The unpleasant smell goes away once the dough is fully baked because the smell is present only when there is moisture. You can find it in Greek and Middle Eastern markets.

1. In a big bowl add the first six ingredients, the liquid ones plus orange zest, and mix well. (In baking, for all practical purposes, sugar is considered liquid).

2. In another bowl add the last six ingredients, the dry ones, and mix thoroughly.

3. Mix the liquid ingredients with the dry ones. Mix as little as possible. The less you work the mixture the lighter and crunchier your cookies will be.

4. Turn the oven to 360°F. Form the cookies in balls and flatten the top or roll the dough 1/2 inch thick and cut with a cookie cutter. I always use the one-inch star cookie cutter because I love how small and cute these melomakarona become. Place them on a cookie sheet and bake for 25 minutes, until golden brown.

5. In the meantime make the syrup. Bring the water, sugar, and orange peel to a boil and let it boil for 5 minutes. Turn the heat off, add the honey and mix.

6. When all the cookies are baked, place them upside down in a big deep pan, as close to each other as possible. Carefully pour the hot syrup on them and let them soak for an hour. Turn the cookies right side up, and leave them in the syrup overnight. In the morning, arrange them on a nice platter, sprinkle with walnuts or pistachios, and drizzle with the rest of the syrup.

French Christmas Cookies (50) 🗹 🌾

These cookies come from France in many variations, depending on the region. I love these particular ones as the combination of orange zest, lemon and almonds is irresistible.

440 grams or 4 1/2 cups almond powder or 4 cups blanched almonds
180 grams or 1 cup dry fruits. I use 1/2 cup glazed orange peel (page 174) and 1/2 cup cranberries
2 teaspoons cinnamon
1/8 teaspoon ground cloves
1 teaspoon pure vanilla extract
Zest of one lemon
3 egg whites
380 grams or 3 cups powdered sugar
A generous pinch of salt
2 tablespoons lemon juice

1. In the bowl of the food processor add the almond powder with the dry fruits, cinnamon, ground cloves, vanilla extract, and the zest of one lemon. Pulse until you have a fine sand consistency. The choice of dry fruits will greatly affect the taste of your cookies. I think that the combination of glazed orange peel and cranberries works very well with almonds. Alternatively, you can use dried pineapple or candied cherries or raisins, or a combination.
2. In a mixer bowl start whisking the egg whites. When they start to froth add the salt and the powdered sugar gradually. When the meringue forms thick peaks, add the lemon juice and whisk some more. Take out 3/4 of a cup of the meringue (NOT 3/4 of the meringue), cover it with plastic wrap, and save it in the fridge for the decoration of the cookies.
3. Fold the almond mixture with the rest of the meringue. It is going to resemble a thick paste rather than cookie dough. With a rolling pin and between two parchment paper sheets spread the mixture into a 1/2-inch thick dough. Start cutting cookies with Christmas cookie cutters and placing them on a cookie sheet lined with parchment paper. I use a rectangular spatula to help me lift the cookies off the counter and onto the cookie sheet. Depending on the size and freshness of your eggs, your dough might be more or less fluffy. The fluffier dough is good for the final texture of the cookies but not for shaping them. If your dough is too fluffy and difficult to shape, place it in the fridge for 30 minutes to facilitate your cookie cutting.
4. Turn the oven to 320°F.
5. When you have finished cutting the cookies, it is time to decorate them with the saved meringue (before you bake them). If your meringue has started to loosen up, whisk it again to regain the stiffness we need for the decoration. Transfer the stiff meringue to a piping bag with a very small nozzle tip and decorate your cookies.
6. Take the decorated cookies to the oven and bake for 15-18 minutes. They are ready when they are not sticking to the parchment paper anymore, and can be easily lifted off the paper. Be attentive. If the meringue decorations start to turn yellow, you will need to lower your oven temperature slightly.
You can save the cookies in an airtight container for weeks.

Pam: Oh my! I was not expecting so much flavor in such a small bite!

Bûche De Noël: Yule Log (*12-14*) 🌾

I do not think that there has been any Christmas day in the last twenty years that I have not made this dessert, whether we are hosting or are invited for the Christmas dinner. I love it!

<u>**Chocolate Base**</u>
180 grams or 6 ounces chocolate
4 egg yolks
100 grams or 1/2 cup sugar
4 egg whites
A generous pinch of salt
<u>**Filling**</u>
300 grams or 1 1/4 cups cream
20 grams or 2 tablespoons powdered sugar
30 grams or 2 tablespoons rum
200 grams or 7 ounces chestnuts in a vacuum package

1. Preheat the oven to 350°F. Line a cookie sheet with parchment paper that is at least 9 x13 inches and butter it.
2. In a Bain Marie or the microwave—very carefully—melt the chocolate.
3. In a bowl whisk the sugar with the 4 egg yolks for 4-5 minutes until the mixture turns lighter in color. Add the melted chocolate and fold in with soft strokes.
4. In a clean and dry mixer bowl, add the 4 egg whites and a pinch of salt and whisk until stiff peaks are formed. Fold the meringue in the chocolate and egg yolk mixture until just incorporated, and spread on the parchment paper, trying to create a neat rectangular shape of 9 x13 inches. I usually load the mixture into a piping bag to create a neat rectangular base.
5. Bake it in the oven for 20 minutes. To check if it is done take it off the oven and check that the base peels off the parchment paper. When it does it is ready.
6. On your kitchen counter, spread a bigger piece of parchment paper (at least 10 x14 inches) and sprinkle a tablespoon of sugar on it. Take the chocolate base out of the oven and place it on the sugared parchment paper upside down. Carefully peel the top paper off the base (the one it baked on) and let the base cool down for ten or fifteen minutes. Remove and discard the top paper and roll the chocolate base with the bottom paper so that it keeps the rolled shape. Leave it on the counter until it cools completely, or even overnight, rolled and covered with a kitchen towel.
7. In a food processor, add all the filling ingredients and process until the mixture thickens up. Unroll the chocolate base and spread the filling on top of the base, as neatly as possible. Roll the base back in the direction it has previously been rolled. Sprinkle with powdered sugar and decorate either with chocolate leaves (page 8) or mushroom meringues and some berries. You can also apply a thin layer of whipped cream onto the Christmas log.
Chocolate Leaves: Melt 50 grams of chocolate. Choose 6-8 beautiful leaves from a plant and wash and dry them thoroughly. With a small brush, apply melted chocolate to the most textured side of each leaf. Place in the fridge to cool and then carefully peel off the green leaf, releasing the chocolate leaf. Keep in the fridge until ready to use.

Marlee: *This dessert was so rich and creamy! I could eat it every day and never be tired of it! It is definitely one of my top three desserts!*

Christmas Pavlova (8-12) 🌾

One of the most impressive desserts, and one of the most irresistible. Pavlova is not complicated but is quite technical as you have to follow some rules. Please read the instructions and rules on page 52.

3 egg whites at room temperature
50 grams or 1/4 cup sugar
90 grams or 3/4 cup powdered sugar
A pinch of salt
5 grams or 1 tablespoon cornstarch
8 grams or 1 tablespoon white vinegar or lemon juice
480 grams or 2 cups heavy cream
250 grams or 1 cup mascarpone or cream cheese
A pinch of salt + 2 tablespoons powdered sugar
30 grams or 2 tablespoons rum (optional)
2 cups fresh fruit of your choice and a few leaves of spearmint

1. In a clean and dry bowl, place the egg whites and start whisking at medium speed. When the eggs start to froth, gradually add the sugar a tablespoon at a time, first the regular and then the powdered, and a pinch of salt. Be very careful in adding the sugar slowly or your meringue will "weep" (undissolved sugar comes out like tears or drops when baking). After you have added all the sugar, turn the speed up slightly to medium-high.
2. Meanwhile turn the oven on to 220°F on the air setting. On parchment paper draw a wreath by drawing two concentric circles (same center), one bigger, 10 inches in diameter, and one smaller, 8 inches in diameter, inside the bigger one. Flip the paper over so that the pencil is on the back and your meringue will not come in contact with it.
3. Back to your meringue. When you lift the whisk up, the peak should be stiff and only slightly lean over, and if you turn the bowl upside down, the meringue should not fall off. Fold in the cornstarch and vinegar in soft movements. Transfer the meringue to a piping bag and pipe out a wreath in curvy strokes on the parchment paper, following your drawing.
4. Place in the oven and bake for 2 or 2 1/2 hours. Keep an eye on it because not all ovens are the same. If your meringue starts to brown, lower the temperature. Leave the pavlova in the oven to cool completely, preferably overnight. When completely cool, remove from the parchment paper and store in an airtight container or place carefully on a platter.
5. When you are ready to serve the pavlova, make this very fancy whipped cream - which is fitting for this beautiful Christmas dessert. Whisk the heavy cream with the mascarpone or cream cheese, salt, powdered sugar, and rum. When the whisk leaves its trail on the cream (medium peak cream), stop whisking and transfer the cream to a piping bag. Decorate the meringue with a nice pattern. Place different kinds of berries neatly on the cream and serve. If you have a good berry sauce or coulis (page 41) drizzle a little on the fruit. Consume within three or four hours of assembling. It will still be tasty the next day, but the meringue will not be crunchy as it starts to absorb moisture after a few hours.

Silas: *This is a fancy dessert!*

Chocolate with chestnuts 🥛 🌾

There are few flavors that yell Christmas more than chestnuts do. They are sweet, comforting, and simultaneously luscious. Exactly what Christmas should feel like!

Filling

200 grams or 7 ounces chestnuts, boiled and peeled. I prefer to use vacuum-packaged French chestnuts which are superb.

80 grams or 6 tablespoons water or milk (see below)

30 grams or 2 tablespoons sugar

30 grams or 2 tablespoons rum

200 grams or 7 ounces dark chocolate

A pinch of salt

You can use milk with your chestnuts, giving them a richer taste, but you compromise shelf-life. The chocolate will have to be consumed within 4-5 days. If you use water, the chocolate will have a longer shelf-life, but supposedly the taste will not be as luscious. I say supposedly because, to be honest, these chocolates are so good that you will not even notice the difference.

1. Place all the filling ingredients in a food processor and mix until you achieve a very smooth cream.

2. Transfer the cream to a pot and cook, stirring constantly, until the filling thickens up to a thick mashed potato consistency. It will take just a few minutes. Cover it with plastic wrap, place it in the fridge, and let the mixture cool completely.

3. Take the chestnut filling out of the fridge and with a small spoon (if you have a spoon that forms fruit balls use it), take a small amount and form it into small balls. Continue until all the chestnut puree is formed into small balls of consistent size.

4. Melt the chocolate and temper it according to the instructions on page 7. Add a pinch of salt.

5. Place a chestnut ball on a fork and dip it in the chocolate. Take it out, tap the fork a couple of times with your finger, and place it on parchment paper to cool and set. Continue with the rest of the filling. For a fancier look, use chocolate molds. After you temper the chocolate, place a small amount of chocolate in every socket of a chocolate mold. Move the dish around to cover the sides. Place a ball of the chestnut puree in every socket. Fill with chocolate and tap the mold lightly to remove any trapped air. Let the chocolate candy set before you unmold it. See page 126 for more detailed instructions on how to use chocolate molds.

Ann: Can I have one of these every day? For the rest of my life?

Fast Glazed Orange Sticks (48) 🍊 🌾

To make glazed orange peels, you need six days, unfortunately. I have given the recipe for the glazed orange peels in my first cookbook. However, there is a faster way to make them and they turn out quite good, given the time invested in them.

2 Oranges
1 cup water (use 1/2 cup water and 1/4 cup sugar for every orange you peel)
1/2 cup sugar
200 grams or 7 ounces chocolate
A pinch of sea salt

1. Peel the oranges by cutting a disc off the top and bottom of the orange. With a sharp paring knife score the peel in 5-6 places from top to bottom to remove the peel from the flesh. After you remove the peel, slice it in 1/8 of an inch thick sticks.

2. To remove the bitterness of the orange peel (a process that takes five days in the original recipe), place the orange sticks in cold water (no sugar), bring them to a boil, and let them boil for two minutes, and drain them. Place them in cold water again. Bring back to a boil, boil them for two minutes, and drain them again. Repeat the process for a third and final time starting with fresh water every time.

3. Now, juice the two oranges and add the juice with the orange peel sticks, 1 cup water, and the sugar in a small pot over very low heat. Let the orange peels simmer until all the liquid has evaporated (around 30 min). Be attentive during the last 5-10 minutes when little water is left. Drain the peels, and arrange them on a rack. Place the rack with the peels in the oven to dry for 30 minutes at 160°F or leave them on the rack for a day at room temperature to dry.

4. In a Bain Marie melt the chocolate and add a pinch of sea salt. Mix to incorporate. Temper the chocolate as explained on page 7. Dip the orange peels in the chocolate, either completely or two-thirds of the way. Place them on parchment paper and leave until the chocolate is set.

Chocolate with Grand Marnier (25) 🥛 🌾

250 grams or 8 ounces dark chocolate
10 grams or 1 tablespoon Grand Marnier or cognac
25 small pieces of Glazed Orange peels
A pinch of sea salt flakes

1. In a Bain Marie melt the chocolate: Place the chocolate in a small metal bowl and place the bowl over a small pot with one cup of water, over low heat and let the water simmer. The chocolate will melt from the steam. Make sure that the bottom of the bowl, where the chocolate is, does not come in contact with the simmering water. Also, steam should not get in contact with the chocolate because the chocolate will be ruined by it (see page 6).

2. When all the chocolate is melted, temper it according to the instructions on page 7.

3. If you are serving children, warm up the Grand Marnie or cognac slightly until it steams. The alcohol will burn out but the wonderful taste will not be lost.

4. Add the Grand Marnier or cognac to the chocolate and mix to incorporate. Mix until the chocolate starts to thicken up. Immediately transfer the chocolate into a piping bag loaded with the tip of your choice, preferably a star tip.

5. On a cookie sheet, place parchment paper. Start creating little circular chocolates on the paper. Decorate with small pieces of Glazed Orange peels and a pinch of sea salt flakes. Let the chocolate cool completely and then remove it from the paper.

Since, both the glazed orange peels and the chocolate are so beautiful, I like to have a bunch of them around the house in small bowls as Christmas decorations.

French Galette des Rois (8-12)

On the first day of the year, Greeks eat a cake called Vasilopita (the "pita" of Saint Vasileios, a Greek theologian and philanthropist) that has a coin hidden inside. Whoever gets the coin gets to enjoy a blessed year! It's a fact. French have a similar tradition: on the sixth of January, when the three wise men traditionally visited Jesus, the French put a small clay figurine, la féve, in a unique dessert and whoever gets it, gets to be the king for that day. Because the French recipe is exquisite, I am giving you the French version. It is also very simple to make.

1 package of ready-made puff pastry (two sheets)
125 grams or 1/2 cup + 2 tablespoons sugar
120 grams or 1 stick butter, room temperature
200 grams or 2 cups almond powder
A generous pinch of salt
2 egg yolks
2 tablespoons rum or cognac or 1 teaspoon vanilla extract
Zest of one orange

1. In a mixer bowl add the sugar and butter and whisk until lighter in color. Whisk the two egg yolks together, take out a tablespoon of the egg yolk and save it in the fridge to brush the top of the dessert later. Add the almond powder, the rest of the two egg yolks, salt, rum, and orange zest, and incorporate. Cover the filling and place it in the fridge for at least one hour to set; otherwise, it will be too runny when baking.
2. Roll out the two puff pastry sheets. Cut two discs, one eleven and one twelve inches in diameter. Place the smaller disk on buttered parchment paper. This is the bottom of the dessert. With your finger apply some water around the edge, so that the top disc will seal.
3. Place the almond filling on the bottom pastry and spread it neatly, leaving a ring with no filling around the edge. Place a small clay figurine or a coin wrapped in aluminum foil in a random spot in the filling.
4. Transfer the other puff pastry dough on top of the filling, pressing the edges of the two pastry sheets together to seal with a fork. Decorate the top by scoring curved lines on top and brush with the tablespoon of the saved egg yolk. Cover with plastic wrap and refrigerate for another 30 minutes to let the filling set. This dessert is easy except for the danger of having the filling spill out of the pastry dough. That is why we need to let it set in the fridge twice.
5. Turn the oven on to 390°F.
6. Take your pastry out of the fridge and bake for 30-35 minutes until golden brown.
Good luck to becoming the queen or king of the day!

Tip: You may use the Almond filling of the Galette des Rois with phyllo dough instead of puff pastry. Layer half of the phyllo in a pan, brushing with butter in between each phyllo, add the filling of the Galette des Rois, add the rest of the phyllo (do not forget to butter each phyllo), and bake this unique baklava. You will end up with a unique and wonderful Baklava (see page 104).

__Allie:__ I loved this dessert because it was the perfect balance of sweet and slightly savory! I could eat this every day!

Choux puffs with Red Caviar (24)

Choux puffs are a versatile and tasty preparation to master. It is festive and is served at parties very often, as it can be made two or three days in advance and assembled very quickly.

100 grams or 1/2 cup water
100 grams or 1/2 cup milk minus 2 tablespoons
1/2 teaspoon sugar
1/2 teaspoon salt
90 grams or 6 tablespoons butter
130 grams or 1 cup flour
4 medium or 3 big eggs
100 grams or 4 ounces parmesan cheese
200 grams or 7 ounces cream cheese
Red Caviar

1. In a medium pot add the water, milk, sugar, salt, and butter (cut in very small pieces because we want the butter to have melted before the liquid starts to boil) and stir to dissolve the salt and sugar. Bring to a boil. Let it boil for 2 minutes and take off the heat. Add the flour all at once, and stir vigorously until it is all absorbed and there are no clumps. Return the pot to the fire and continue stirring until the dough turns into a ball and a film of dough is formed at the bottom of the pan. Remove from the heat.

2. Place the dough in a mixer bowl with the kneading hook and start stirring slowly. Turn the oven to 375°F.

3. A few minutes later, when the dough has cooled down a little, start adding the eggs, one at a time, while still stirring. Wait for each egg to be incorporated into the dough before you add the next one. When the eggs are thoroughly absorbed, the dough should look shiny and elastic. It should still be firm, and the markings of the kneading hook should stay visible. If you feel that the dough starts to loosen up too much do not add the last egg. Stir for a few more minutes and turn the mixer off.

4. Add the parmesan, grated finely, to the dough and mix well.

5. Transfer the dough to a piping bag with a nozzle of around 1/4 of an inch diameter. Place parchment paper on a cookie sheet, butter it lightly, and start piping, creating small discs and then building up a second row on top of the first as you go. This way your choux will have room to puff up nicely. Bake for 30 minutes until golden brown and then open the oven door briefly and with your sharpest knife prick the top of every pastry once to allow the trapped moisture to escape, so that they do not collapse later (do not open the oven door before the 30 minutes). Let the choux bake for 5-10 more minutes and take them out of the oven.

6. Let the choux cool completely. At this point, you may store them for a few days in an air-tight container. Before you are ready to serve, open them up with a sharp knife and spread a tablespoon of cream cheese in each one, or place the cream cheese on top of the choux. Decorate with Red Caviar and place on a nice platter.

Easter

Hamali from Alonissos *(or fried baklava)*

More than twenty years ago we visited a breathtakingly beautiful Greek island called Alonissos. I tried this dessert, which is a local delicacy and I was blown away. I got the recipe from a kind lady and it stayed safely hidden in my recipe book all these years until I started writing this cookbook. Because the filling has to rest for five whole days, and then five more for the flavors to infuse I kept postponing making this dessert. Please don't be like me! Make the filling and wait for five days to roll the Hamali and then five more days till you try them. I promise they are worth the waiting, Plan ahead to have them ready for Easter.

3 cups finely chopped walnuts
1 cup fine semolina or Cream of Wheat (not the instant type)
2 tablespoons cinnamon
1/2 teaspoon ground cloves
1/4 teaspoon nutmeg
1 1/2 cups honey

1 package of phyllo dough
1/2 cup of powdered sugar
Vegetable oil for frying (sunflower works well)

1. Mix the chopped walnuts with semolina and spices. Add the honey and mix well. Place the mixture in a bowl, cover it with plastic wrap and let it rest for five days. The flavors will infuse and the semolina will absorb the honey and become deliciously moist and aromatic.

2. On day 5, cut the phyllo dough into 4 inch wide strips. Place a walnut-sized ball of filling on a phyllo strip, press it to flatten it slightly, and roll the phyllo dough either like a spring roll or in a triangle to create a fortune cookie shape. Then turn the edges of the triangle inward. Make sure that either way you roll the phyllo dough, the edges are flipped in, enclosing the filling completely. If you roll them like spring roll after two rolls fold the long edges in to seal the filling and then continue rolling.

3. Fry the hamali in hot vegetable oil until just golden. Transfer them to kitchen paper to drain the excess oil. Leave them on clean kitchen paper for another five days. Store in an airtight container at room temperature. Before you serve, sprinkle them with powdered sugar.

Enjoy!

Melitinia from Santorini (60)

An undoubtedly unforgettable pastry that is quite time-consuming to make. This dessert comes from beautiful Santorini, and the tradition is that the women of Santorini gather together in groups on Tuesday of Holy Week and in a line production mode, make this dessert. It is truly a gastronomic and cultural treasure.

A complicating factor is that two ingredients, the Anthotyro cheese and the Mastic gum, are unique Greek products and therefore hard to find elsewhere. But there are alternatives: Anthotyro can be substituted with Ricotta cheese and Mastic with orange zest. Mastic gum can be ordered through apollogum.com (see note on page 67).

Dough
2 tablespoons olive oil
1 tablespoon vinegar
1 cup water
3 cups flour
Filling
4 cups of Anthotyro OR Ricotta
5 pearls of Mastic OR zest of an orange
3 cups sugar
1 egg
1 teaspoon vanilla extract
1 teaspoon baking powder
2 cups flour

1. Start by mixing the olive oil, vinegar, and water. Slowly add the flour, a little at a time. Knead the dough, and stop adding flour as soon as the dough is still soft but no longer sticky. It should take around 3 cups of flour. Knead for 4-5 minutes, pressing the dough with your palm, pushing it away from you, folding it in on itself, and then turning it 45 degrees. Cover the dough with a towel and let it rest for 30 minutes.

2. In a food processor, add 1 cup sugar and the Mastic or orange zest. Work until the Mastic (or orange zest) is completely dissolved. Add the cheese and mix briefly, just until smooth.

3. Add the rest of the sugar, egg, and vanilla to the food processor until you have a creamy, homogeneous mixture. Finally, add the flour and baking powder and pulse until incorporated. Fill a piping bag with the mixture and cover the rest with a wet towel.

4. Turn the oven to 380°F. Divide the dough into four balls. Roll one out as thin as you possibly can. Dust your working surface with flour or the dough will stick. With a round cutter that is at least 3 inches in diameter, cut circles. With the piping bag, pipe out a disc of the cheese filling on the dough leaving the outer half-inch ring without filling, as shown above.

5. Lift one disc and hold it in your left palm while you pinch with your right hand, around the perimeter. Place it on a lightly buttered cookie sheet and continue with the second Melitini. When you fill up the first cookie sheet, take a wet tablespoon and level the top of each melitini. Take the cookie sheet to the oven and bake for 20 minutes until golden brown. Continue with forming and baking the rest of the dough and cheese filling.

An **easier version** of this unforgettable dessert can be made using the phyllo dough of the Pastel de Nata (page 150, step 4) and making a filling with Ricotta cheese. Add **2 cups ricotta cheese + 1 1/2 cup sugar + 1 cup flour + 1 teaspoon baking powder + zest of half an orange + 1 teaspoon vanilla + a pinch of salt and half an egg.**

Panna Cotta (12-16) 🌾

My mom's friend Mrs. Popi is married to an Italian. For many decades, they owned one of the best Italian restaurants in Greece. She was so kind to let me have their unique recipe, and share it with you, for this iconic Italian dessert! I am deeply grateful.

750 grams or 3 cups heavy cream
240 grams or 1 cup milk
1 teaspoon vanilla extract
10 egg whites
10 tablespoons white sugar
Topping
3/4 cup brown sugar OR
1/2 cup frozen red fruit with 1/4 cup sugar and a few fresh berries

1. Heat the heavy cream with the milk and the vanilla until it steams; remove from heat. Let it cool slightly. You may use just cream (1000 grams) for a fuller taste, but this lighter version is excellent.

2. Turn the oven to 350°F. Choose a cake form, either rectangular or a round bundt form or small individual ones. Place in the oven another bigger pan and fill it with enough water so that the cake form fits in the bigger pan and the water comes up almost to the level of the panna cotta.

3. Mix the egg whites with the sugar well, but do not whisk.

4. If you want to serve with caramel, melt the brown sugar in a heavy saucepan over medium heat until it starts to melt, turning into caramel. Swirl the saucepan around slightly until all the sugar melts and takes an amber color. Be careful that your caramel does not turn brown. Control the heat by lifting the pan off the stove briefly so that the caramel melts completely but does not darken too much. (Read instructions on caramel making on page 8). Pour the caramel at the bottom of the cake form. Be very careful with caramel as it is extremely hot and will cause severe burns if you touch it.

5. Add the egg whites to the cream, mix well, and transfer to the cake form or small forms.

6. Place the form with the panna cotta in the pan or arrange the small forms in the pan with the water and take the pan to the oven to bake as in a Bain Marie setting. Let the Panna Cotta bake for 40-50 minutes if it is a big one or 30 minutes if you are using small forms until a knife inserted comes out clean.

7. Let the cream cool completely and place it in the fridge for at least 3 hours or preferably overnight. If you did not make caramel, place red fruit with sugar in a small pot and cook for five minutes. Unmold the Panna Cotta on a platter and decorate with the red fruit.

Tip: If you unmold the Panna Cotta too soon, most of the caramel will be stuck at the bottom of the form. If you wait overnight, the caramel will be all dissolved (or almost all) and it will dress the Panna Cotta wonderfully.

Alex: The creaminess of this thing....out of this world!

Natasa's lemon yogurt tart (12)

My signature dessert is a light and refreshing lemon yogurt you can make very quickly and eat with any meal. On Easter day, you can add a little gelatin to the yogurt and make it into small, fancy tartelettes. Alternatively, you can use the easier tart shells described on step 4 of page 150, as holders for the yogurt filling.

Another way to enjoy the lemon yogurt is to melt 3 ounces or 100 grams of **chocolate** and add it to the yogurt drop by drop while stirring constantly. Thin flakes of wonderful chocolate will form in the cool lemony yogurt.

<u>**Tart or Tartelettes**</u>
200 grams or 1 1/2 cups flour
1 tablespoon vinegar
1/2 teaspoon salt
1 stick or 1/2 cup unsalted butter, cold
2 tablespoons milk, cold
Extra butter for the pan
<u>**Lemon Yogurt**</u>
2 pounds of Greek yogurt, 2% or 5%, or whole-fat yogurt. Do NOT use 0%.
1 can or 14 ounces of sweetened condensed milk
2 lemons, zest, and juice (about 1/2 cup lemon juice)
2 gelatin sheets or 2 teaspoons of gelatin powder

1. Add the flour, vinegar, salt, and cold butter to a food processor and pulse until all the butter is incorporated. Add two tablespoons of cold milk and pulse again. Check that the dough holds together. Remove immediately, form it into a ball, flatten it (to facilitate the rolling into a pie crust later), wrap it up in plastic wrap, and place in the fridge for at least thirty minutes.

2. Preheat the oven to 375°F. Take the dough out of the fridge, place it between two parchment papers, and roll it out. Place the rolled dough in a big, buttered, round pie shell and bake for about 30 minutes. Alternatively, you can cut small discs (2.5 to 3.5 inches in diameter) and place them in small individual tartelettes that you have buttered. Prick with a fork, and fill them with clean, dry beans to help them keep their shape when baked. Bake for 10 minutes, depending on their size, remove the beans and bake for 3-4 more minutes. Let them cool completely before you unmold them.

3. Make the lemon yogurt: Wash the lemons very well in hot water to remove any wax that is coating the peel. Zest two lemons and juice them.

4. In a bowl add the yogurt and condensed milk and mix. Add the zest and lemon juice a little at a time. You might need the juice of just one lemon or you might need three, depending on how juicy and how sour your lemon is. Taste the mixture. It has to be wonderfully lemony to balance the sweetness of the milk. This is the lemon yogurt.

5. Take 2 gelatin sheets or 2 teaspoons of gelatin powder and soak them in a little water according to the instructions on page 6. Three or four minutes later, warm 1/4 cup of water and dissolve the gelatin in it. Mix dissolved gelatin with the lemon yogurt until very well incorporated. Let it cool for 30 minutes and then transfer it to the tart or tartelettes.

Courtney: *Lemon yogurt is like sunshine on a cloudy day*

Meringue with Hazelnuts *(10)* 🌾

Please read the detailed instructions on meringue making on page 52.

Meringue
3 egg whites
125 grams or 1 cup powdered sugar
5 grams or 1 tablespoon cornstarch
1 tablespoon white wine vinegar
110 grams or 1 cup hazelnut, finely ground
Ganache
120 grams or 1/2 cup cream
120 grams or 4 ounces dark chocolate
1/2 teaspoon vanilla extract
A pinch of salt
Caramel for Decoration: 1 cup sugar plus a pinch of salt
Hazelnuts for decoration

1. In a clean mixer bowl, place the egg whites and start whisking at medium speed. When they start to froth, begin adding the sugar a tablespoon at a time. Turn the speed up slightly to medium-high as soon as all the sugar is added.

2. Turn the oven to 220°F on the air setting. On parchment paper trace with a pencil a 9-inch circle, or small individual ones, rounds, or squares. Flip the paper over so that the pencil marking is on the back and your meringue will not come in contact with it.

3. Turn the mixer off once the meringue is thick enough and when you turn the bowl upside down, the meringue does not move. Fold in the cornstarch, vinegar, and powdered hazelnuts in soft movements.

4. Transfer on the parchment paper, either with a piping bag or with a spatula, and form in any shape you desire: nests, hearts, flat disks, heaps, or pyramids following your drawing. Place in the oven and bake for 2 1/2 hours if it is one big meringue, or 1 1/2 hours if they are small ones. If your meringue starts to turn yellow during baking, you need to turn your oven down to 200°F. Leave the meringue in the oven to cool completely. When completely cool, remove the meringue from the parchment paper and store it in an airtight container or place it carefully on a platter.

5. On the day you will serve the dessert, make the Ganache. Chop the chocolate in a bowl. In a pot, heat the cream, and add the vanilla and a pinch of salt. Remove from heat once it starts to steam. Add to the chocolate, wait for two minutes for the chocolate to soften, and then start stirring with a spatula until the chocolate is completely melted and incorporated into the cream. Cover with a kitchen towel and let it cool for about one hour before you use it.

6. In a small heavy saucepan, add the sugar over medium heat. Once the sugar starts to melt, swirl the pan around ever so slightly. Control the heat by pulling the saucepan off the burner and then returning it, until a blonde, brownish caramel is achieved. Turn the heat off and let the caramel cool slightly (see page 8). Take a few hazelnuts, prick them with a toothpick, dip them in the caramel, and let them drip onto parchment paper. An easy way is to attach the

toothpick with duct tape to one of your cupboards. Pour the rest of the caramel on parchment paper to cool and be used for decoration. Be careful because caramel is very hot.

7. On the hazelnut meringue spread the chocolate ganache and decorate with the caramel hazelnuts and the broken caramel chunks. Sprinkle with salt and serve.

Contents

Printed in the USA
CPSIA information can be obtained
at www.ICGtesting.com
LVHW061959261123
764902LV00090B/576